POEMS TO ENJOY: BOOK FIVE

Chosen and Edited by Verner Bickley

Proverse Hong Kong

VERNER BICKLEY, MBE, PhD, is a well-known "voice", educationist, and adjudicator, who has held director-level positions in Universities and Government Departments. He is Chairman of the English-Speaking Union (HK) and Co-Founder of the International Proverse Prize for unpublished writing. He travels frequently to judge public-speaking competitions and regularly adjudicates verse and prose speaking and reading, as well as drama and choral speaking.

Dr Bickley's series of graded poetry anthologies – **POEMS TO ENJOY** – is a well-established tool for learning and teaching English at all levels. Useful notes and a teaching guide are also included.

Taken as a whole, this five-book series is suitable for all students, teachers and parents. **Book 1** can be used and enjoyed by children under five up to about ten years old; **Book 2** by children from about age seven to twelve; **Book 3** by intermediate readers from about ten to fourteen years old; **Book 4** by intermediate to advanced readers from about fourteen to sixteen yeras old; and **Book 5** by intermediate and advanced students from about fifteen years old and above. Students, parents and teachers will enjoy and find useful Dr Bickley's selection of poems.

Parents will welcome this book, which gives them the opportunity to read aloud with their children.

POEMS TO ENJOY

BOOK FIVE

AN ANTHOLOGY OF POEMS

FOR INTERMEDIATE and ADVANCED
STUDENTS AND READERS

WITH TEACHING AND LEARNING NOTES AND GUIDE

**CHOSEN AND EDITED BY DR VERNER BICKLEY,
MBE, PhD (Lond.), MA, BA (Hons), DipEd, LRAM,
LGSM, FCIL, FRSA**

Proverse Hong Kong

Poems to Enjoy: Book Five
Chosen and Edited by Verner Bickley
and with teaching notes by Verner Bickley
(no accompanyting audio recording).
Copyright © Verner Bickley, June 2016.
4th edition, published in Hong Kong by Proverse Hong Kong, June 2016.
ISBN: 978-988-8228-52-2
Available from: https://createspace.com/6348861

Poems to Enjoy: Book Five, 3rd edition,
with teaching notes by Verner Bickley and accompanying audio recording,
with readers, Verner Bickley and Gillian Bickley,
published in Hong Kong by Proverse Hong Kong, April 2015.
Copyright © Verner Bickley, April 2015.
ISBN: 978-988-8167-49-4

Third Edition distribution:
(Hong Kong and worldwide): The Chinese University Press of Hong Kong,
The Chinese University of Hong Kong, Shatin, New Territories, Hong Kong SAR.
E-mail: cup-bus@cuhk.edu.hk   Web site: www.chineseupress.com
(United Kingdom): Enquiries and orders to Christine Penney, Stratford-upon-Avon, Warwickshire
CV37 6DN, England. Email: <chrisp@proversepublishing.com>

Enquiries: Proverse Hong Kong, P. O. Box 259, Tung Chung Post Office, Tung Chung,
Lantau Island, NT, Hong Kong, SAR, China.
E-mail: proverse@netvigator.com   Web site: www.proversepublishing.com

Illustrations copyright © Proverse Hong Kong.
Cover design, Proverse Hong Kong and Artist Hong Kong Company.

The right of Verner Bickley to be identified as the anthologiser and editor of this work has been asserted by him in accordance with the Copyright, Designs and Patents Act 1988.

All rights reserved. No part of this publication may be reproduced, stored in a retrieval system, or transmitted, in any form or by any means, electronic, mechanical, photocopying, recording or otherwise, without the prior written permission of the publisher. The book is sold subject to the condition that it shall not, by way of trade or otherwise, be lent, re-sold, hired out or otherwise circulated without the publisher's prior written consent in any form of binding or cover other than that in which it is published and without a similar condition including this condition being imposed on the subsequent owner or purchaser. Please contact Proverse Hong Kong in writing, to request any and all permissions (including but not restricted to republishing, inclusion in anthologies, translation, reading, performance and use as set pieces in examinations and festivals).

Poems to Enjoy, Book Five was first published in the United Kingdom in 1960, by University of London Press Ltd (ISBN 0 340 07585 6) copyright © Verner Bickley 1960, with Teaching Notes in a separate volume. Copyright © Verner Bickley 1960.
About half of the poems in both the 3rd (and 1st) edition of *Poems to Enjoy, Book Five*, were included in the 2nd edition of this work, *Poems to Enjoy Book 3*, part of a three-book series.

Proverse Hong Kong

British Library Cataloguing in Publication Data (for 3rd edition)

Poems to enjoy.
Book 5. -- 3rd ed.
1. English poetry. 2. Oral interpretation of poetry
3. English poetry--Study and teaching
(Secondary) 4. English language--Study and teaching--
Foreign speakers.
I. Bickley, Verner Courtenay.
821'.008-dc23

ISBN-13: 9789888167494

Poems to Enjoy, Book Five (4th Ed, 2015)   4

INTRODUCTION

TO ALL STUDENTS

Poetry is an interesting and special way of expressing human thoughts and feelings. Many poems tell a story, others express a mood and some describe a scene. A large number of poems must be read aloud to be fully enjoyed.

For this reason, **Part One** of this book contains poems which are especially suitable for speaking, either by individuals, or by groups arranged in different ways. Whatever the treatment, as the title of the book implies, the main purpose is enjoyment and this same purpose applies equally to all parts of this book.

Each of the poems in **Part Two** paints a picture in words and describes persons, animals and scenes, many of which you will find familiar. The pictures you see in your mind's eye when listening to the poems can be sketched or painted after you have listened to the poems.

All the poems in **Part Three** are narrative poems, poems which tell a story. After you have read these poems yourself or perhaps after a reading by your teacher or one or both of your parents, a discussion will usually help to clear up any difficulties.

I hope that the experience of poetry that you will gain from reading the poems in this book will encourage you to attempt to write poetry yourself. Not only can this be an interesting venture, but it can also help you to improve your ability to write the English language more effectively.

TO ALL PARENTS

It is pleasant to share interests and time with children. Poetry is often regarded as difficult. Some is difficult and some is not difficult. The poems in this series are carefully graded, with adequate notes to make reading pleasant and understanding accessible at levels suitable for each reader. Whether or not parents are already in the habit of reading poetry in English, they can enjoy reading the poems in this series of five books, with their children of all ages.

TO ALL TEACHERS

This book contains a variety of poems of different degrees of difficulty to suit different ways of learning. The poems in Part One are suitable for reading aloud; those in Part Two are largely descriptive; and each poem in Part Three tells a story. The sequence in which the poems are used is, however, at the teacher's discretion.

The poems can be used as supplementary reading material, for oral work, including practice of stress and rhythm, and for different kinds of listening activities. The descriptive poems should develop and challenge the students' imagination and the 'story' or 'narrative' poems are included because all students like to hear or read a good story, provided that they can understand it. In addition to being enjoyed for themselves, the narrative poems provide material for choral work, for dramatization, discussions and questioning.

All the poems in this collection are suitable for extra-curricular work, for example, verse-speaking, choral-speaking, drama, and words and movement.

Poetry can be integrated successfully with the presentation and practice or activities stage of an English lesson, and if emphasis is placed on enjoyment and the students are encouraged to participate fully in the lesson, it can make learning more effective. Poetry develops and broadens the imagination through role-playing, provides training in visual perception, helps in the formation of ideas, and adds a new dimension to group work.

Poetry is an exploration of the possibilities of language which can help the student to construct a new and different framework from that of his own language, acquire different sequences and make forward guesses.

GROUPING OF POEMS

Poems to Speak

This section contains poems which have a pronounced rhythmic and musical quality and which are suitable for reading aloud, whether individually, or in chorus, or groups. Because it requires good breath-control, clear enunciation of consonants and precise shaping of vowels, choral speech is valuable as a way of training both ear and voice for all types of solo-speech. Whether a poem should be spoken by the class as a whole, by soloists, or by different groups of various sizes, depends upon the teacher's own preferences, and, even better, upon the ideas of the students themselves. When groups are required, it is a good idea to keep them constant for choral work in different lessons. In this way, it is possible to distribute the ablest speakers in the class among the various groups.

Some suggestions for choral arrangements are given in the Teaching/Learning Guide at the end of the book. Each poem which is at all suitable for choral work is, of course, open to much variation and the suggestions in the Guide should not therefore be taken as obligatory.

Pictures in Poetry
The poems in this section are intended to enhance the students' ability to visualise, in one form or another, what has been described. If the classroom environment is suitable, two or three poems can sometimes be read to create the right atmosphere for a lesson in which the aim is to encourage the students to sketch from the imagination. Once this atmosphere is achieved, the work can begin. When it is complete, the final results can be collected from individuals and shown to the rest of the group or class. Eventually, the students can be encouraged to make their own anthologies by writing out some of the poems from this collection and illustrating them from their own creative work. Pictures and photographs that are similar to scenes in the poems can be brought to the class to be used as the basis for discussion.

The Poet as Storyteller
The poems in this section can be used as material upon which the students can comment and which they can use as the basis for writing their own stories in prose or verse on related themes. The success of the poetry-writing lesson will depend primarily upon the classroom atmosphere; and interruptions from outside the room should, therefore, be avoided as much as is possible. In the concluding stages of each lesson, the students can read their own poems aloud and be invited to make suggestions and comments.

The Teaching and Learning Notes and Guide
The Teaching and Learning Notes and Guide contain suggestions for choral arrangements; definitions and explanations of words and phrases; suggestions for illustration work and story-writing and questions for discussion.

Timeless and traditional
The books contain traditional and timeless poems, as well as poems that inform us how children and adults thought at different periods of time, including at an earlier period of technological sophistication.

The Moral and General Education embodied in the Poems
As in this five-book anthology as a whole, individual poems in *Poems to Enjoy: Book Five* express and model many emotions – tenderness, amusement, admiration, wonder, sadness – and elicit many others – sympathy, concern. Some of the descriptive poems express and teach observation and appreciation of the human and natural world.

Listed below are various points, embodied in individual poems, which can be used as a starting point for class or other discusion, written response, and/or personal consideration. Although many points are listed, they are not comprehensive and much additional food for thought can be found by readers and students themselves.

Human Life
Descriptive summary of the different stages of human life ('Jaques' Seven Ages of Man');

Mystic Experience: 'Kubla Khan'; 'La Belle Dame Sans Merci'.

Love, devotion, loyalty, innocence, modesty, keeping a promise, providing for ones family
The love of a son for his mother and of a mother for her son ('Helen's Tower');
Self-sacrificing romantic love ('The Highwayman');
Romantic love ('Meeting at Night');

Misplaced love and its dangers ('La Belle Dame Sans Merci');
Passionate attachment to another person ('Art Thou Gone in Haste?');
'All for Love' shows devotion and the value of devotion returned;
'The Cap and Bells' tells a story in which devoted persistence gains the loved one.
Loyalty ('Jaffàr').
The innocence of childhood ('The Belfry') and of female adulthood ('She Walks in Beauty').
The value of modesty ('On a Certain Lady at Court').
The duty to keep a promise ('The Listeners'); the duty to provide for ones family ('The Eastern Gate').

Sadness and nostalgia
The sadess of mourning ('Funeral Song', 'The High Song', 'Full Fathom Five', 'Break, Break, Break').
The nostalgia of a person living away from his native land ('The Bells of Shandon', 'The Soldier', *'From* "My Lost Youth"');
Nostalgia for those passed away ('Song of Three Gorges').

The emotions provoked by war: Admiration of a leader for his stoicism and leadership. ('The Death of Admiral Benbow').

The immorality of war: ('After Blenheim')

Politics and history: ('Marching Along'; 'The Bowmen of Shu').

Repetitive work and the exploitation of the individual craftsman
The dulling impact of repetitive manual work and the healing power of music ('The Release');
The boredom of repetitive clerical work ('The Ice-Cart');
The exploitation of the skilled work of the individual craftsman ('The Shawl').

Noise pollution ('The Blacksmiths').

The sea and life at sea in the days of sailing-ships: various perspectives
Working Song ('Sea Shanty');
The courage and sacrifice of seafarers ('One Friday Morn');
Difficult relationships between seafarers ('Old Joe is dead');
Difficulties of communication with loved ones when at sea ('Song');
Fascination with the sea ('On the Sea');
The mystery of the sea ('The Galley of Count Arnaldos');
The romance of sea-board life ('Song from the Ship');
Exploration of a mermaid's desires ('The Mermaid').

A simple life
The pleasures of a simple life ('His Grange, or Private Wealth', 'The Kingfisher');
The rewards of contented honest labour contrasted with the anxiety of ambition ('The Happy Heart');
The sickness caused by idle power is healed by helpful labour ('The Enchanted Shirt').

Leisure activities ('Hunting Song').

Description and evaluation of a person or type of person and lessons drawn from their behaviour
Done with humour ('The Village Schoolmaster');
Possibly with regret ('Parting at Morning').
The price of independence ('The Gipsy Laddie');
Different and misplaced priorities ('Get up and Bar the Door').

Animals
Attachment to a companion animal ('Madrigal'); Spontaneous feelings of benevolence towards creatures (*'From* "The Rime of the Ancient Mariner"').
Sympathy for a working animal ('Poor Old Horse', written from the perspective of an old horse, already retired); for a parrot captive in a country far different from his own ('The Parrot: A True Story').
Amusement and empathy for a kitten playing with leaves ('The Kitten and the Falling Leaves');

Admiration of wild horses ('Horses on the Camargue'); for the skill of creatures which can surpass that of man ('Artists').

Culture
Cultures of the past (the sadness and longing for home of the Bowmen of Shu ('Song of the Bowmen of Shu'); the means of communication available in the pre-technological world ('The Bell-man'));
The power of translation to convey an ancient world to modern readers ('On first looking into Chapman's Homer');
The desire to experience other worlds ('Fragment', 'The Music of the Sea');
The "Seize the day" motif understood by many cultures ('Oh Mistress Mine');
The pleasure given by a cultural festival ('A Feast of Lanterns');
A rebuttal of traditional teaching ('Song of Three Gorges');
Consciousness of continuity even as one culture dies and another grows ('Ode');
The value of harmony, peace and interdependence ('A Morisco').

Philosophy
The cumulative power of ideas when expressed in seductive and powerful language ('Ode').

Use of Language; Technique; Poetic Form

Alliteration
Today, rhyme is given more emphasis than alliteration, which is nevertheless still an important poetic tool. 'The Blacksmiths', a modern version of a poem from the Middle Ages, illustrates how the emphasis then was on alliteration rather than rhyme.

Rhythm and Rhyme
Book Five includes some poems which are particularly strong in rhythm and rhyme (e.g. 'Tarantella', 'Marching Along', 'The Destruction of Sennacherib').

Repetition appears in several poems, including as a refrain (e.g. 'Sea Shanty') and to drive the narrative structure ('The Maid of the Moor').

Description: Many of the poems give descriptions of setting, while their focus is on, for example, a story, or an individual. 'Docks' focuses on the description itself, being an accomplished and very detailed description of dockyards.

Matching of form and subject are entirely the choice of the writer. The decision to follow the conventions of a particular poetic form or otherwise is also the choice of the writer.

Lyrics and narrative poems do not dictate the form of a poem to the extent that, for example, a sonnet (which consists of fourteen iambic pentametres and uses various rhyming patterns – *Please see "Explanation of Selected Terms"*) does.

A classic **sonnet** ('Ozymandias') demonstrates that concern with poetic form and excellence in using it can be fused with poignant observation and a deep moral.

'I Stood Tiptoe' also follows the sonnet form to describe an early morning scene. (A similar topic is described in *'From* "Pippa Passes"', but not in sonnet form.)

Blank verse usually has any number of iambic pentameters, with no rhyme at the end of lines).
Poems in blank verse in Book Five describe, for example, the emotions of a bull in the mating season ('The Bull'), the death of Samson (*'From* "Samson Agonistes"'), the combat between David and Goliath ('Goliath') and that between Sohrab and Rustum ('Sohrab and Rustum').

Narrative poems.
Some of the narrative poems have been well-known and popular for well over a hundred years (e.g. 'The Lady of Shallott'). 'How They Brought the Good News from Ghent to Aix' describes what seems to be, but was not an actual historical event and some demonstrate a type of patriotism (e.g. 'Marching Along').

At least one of the narrative poems has a very direct moral: wickedness will be punished ('Bishop Hatto').

One of the poems in Book Five has been a favourite choice for poetry-speaking competitions for many decades because of its narrative line of subconscious wish-fulfilment, its use of assonance, alliteration, rhythm, the opportunities it gives for changes of pace, tone and mood, its communication of sensual emotions and the wonderful ending ('The Ice-Cart').

Making connections
One poem cleverly links a description of the sun at different times of day with the lives of the people and creatures who live in a specific location ('An Indian Summer on the Prairie').

Another draws philosophy from a careful description of a tropical storm at sea ('Tropic Rain').

***

The audio recording
There is an audio recording of all poems in this collection, read by two adult English native-speakers who enjoy reading poems aloud. Search online for availability of this audio-recording, including in the 3rd edition of *Poems to Enjoy*.

Write to us!
Teachers, students and parents are encouraged to write to us to share their experiences. We would be very interested to know which approach was most useful to you and with what particular poems this was true.
The Proverse website, proversepublishing.com makes provision for you to contact us with your comments.

ACKNOWLEDGEMENTS

For permission to use copyright material, thanks are due to: Messrs. Wm. Blackwood & Sons Ltd. for 'The Highwayman' by Alfred Noyes; Messrs. Allen & Unwin Ltd. for 'The Lychee,' translated by Arthur Waley; to Mrs. Ann Wolfe for 'The High Song' taken from *Requiem* by Humbert Wolfe; to Messrs. Ernest Benn Ltd. for 'The Shawl' by W. Kean Seymour to Messrs. Curtis Brown Ltd. for 'The Horses on the Camargue' by Roy Campbell; to Messrs. A. D. Peters for 'Tarantella' by Hilaire Belloc; to Mrs. W. B. Yeats and Messrs. Macmillan & Co. Ltd. for the poem 'The Cap and Bells' from *Collected Poems of W. B. Yeats;* to Messrs. Macmillan & Co. Ltd. and the Trustees of the Hardy Estate for 'The Garden Seat' taken from *Collected Poems of Thomas Hardy;* to Messrs. Macmillan & Co. Ltd. and Mr. Wilfrid Gibson for 'The Ice Cart' and 'The Release'; to Messrs. Constable & Co. Ltd. for 'The Eastern Gate' from *170 Chinese Poems* by Arthur Waley; to The Literary Trustees of Walter de la Mare for 'Goliath' and 'The Listener'; to The Society of Authors and Mrs. Cicely Binyon for 'The Belfry' by Lawrence Binyon; to Messrs. The Macmillan Company, New York for 'An Indian Summer Day on the Prairie' from *Collected Poems* by Vachel Lindsay; to Messrs. John Murray for 'Song of Three Gorges' by Lu Yu, 'Rain at Dawn' by Po Chu-i and 'A Feast of Lanterns' by Yuan Mei, these poems being taken from *A Feast of Lanterns* in the *Wisdom of the East* series; to Jonathan Cape Ltd. and Mrs. H. M. Davies for 'The Kingfisher' from *The Collected Poems of W. H. Davies;* and to Dr Ezra Pound for 'The Song of the Bowmen of Shu'.

In certain cases it has not been possible to trace the copyright holders. Full acknowledgement of any rights not mentioned here will be made in subsequent editions if notification is received.

CONTENTS

Introduction   5
Acknowledgements   14

PART ONE: POEMS TO SPEAK

TITLE	AUTHOR	PAGE
Funeral Song	Anon.	20
Morisco	Jasper Fisher	21
Art Thou Gone in Haste?	Elizabethan Lyric	22
The Blacksmiths	Anon. (Modernised by K. Sisam)	23
Hunting Song	Henry Fielding	24
Madrigal	Thomas Weekes	25
The Death of Admiral Benbow	Anon.	26
Sea Shanty	Traditional	28
Old Joe is Dead and Gone to Hell	Sea Shanty	28
One Friday Morn	Old Shanty	30
Tarantella	Hilaire Belloc	32
The High Song *From* 'Requiem'	Humbert Wolfe	34
Full Fathom Five	William Shakespeare	35
O Mistress Mine	William Shakespeare	35
The Gipsy Laddie	Folk Song	36
His Grange, or Private Wealth	Robert Herrick	38
The Garden Seat	Thomas Hardy	39
The Bell-Man	Robert Herrick	39
Poor Old Horse	Anon.	40
Song from the Ship (*From* Death's Jest-Book)	T. L. Beddoes	41
Song	Charles Sackville, Earl of Dorset	41
The Maid of the Moor	Anon. (*Modernised by K. Sisam*)	44
The Happy Heart	Thomas Dekker	45
All For Love	Lord Byron	46
The Bells of Shandon	Francis Mahoney	46
The Three Wise Men of Gotham	T. L. Peacock	49
Ode	Arthur O'Shaughnessy	50

Title	Author	Page
Marching Along	Robert Browning	51
Song of the Bowmen of Shu	Ezra Pound	52
An Indian Summer on the Prairie	Vachel Lindsay	53

PART TWO: PICTURES IN POETRY

TITLE	AUTHOR	PAGE
Jacques' Seven Ages of Man	William Shakespeare	56
Break, Break. Break	Alfred, Lord Tennyson	57
Tropic Rain	Robert Louis Stevenson	58
Ozymandias	Percy Bysshe Shelley	59
The Ice-Cart	W.W. Gibson	59
The Listeners	Walter de la Mare	61
On First Looking into Chapman's Homer	John Keats	62
Docks	Dorothy Wellesley	63
Song of Three Gorges	Lu Yu	65
Fragment	John Clare	65
The Lychee	Wang I (*Translated from the Chinese by Arthur Waley*)	66
The Music of the Sea	Thomas Hood	66
The Kingfisher	W. H. Davies	67
The Village Schoolmaster	Oliver Goldsmith	68
The Kitten and the Falling Leaves	William Wordsworth	69
I Stood Tiptoe	John Keats	70
From 'Pippa Passes'	Robert Browning	71
Helen's Tower	Alfred, Lord Tennyson	71
From 'The Rime of the Ancient Mariner'	S. T. Coleridge	72
The Bull (*From* 'The Seasons')	James Thomson	73
On the Sea	John Keats	74
The Belfry	Lawrence Binyon	75
Horses on the Camargue	Roy Campbell	76
She Walks in Beauty	Lord Byron	78
The Kraken	Alfred, Lord Tennyson	79
A Feast of Lanterns	Yuan Mei	80
The Nile	Leigh Hunt	80
The Release	W. W. Gibson	81
Rain at Dawn	Po Chu-i	81
Artists (*From* 'Instinctive Genius and Diligence')	James Hurdis	82

PART THREE: THE POET AS STORYTELLER

TITLE	AUTHOR	PAGE
The Lady of Shalott	Alfred, Lord Tennyson	84
Old Man Travelling	William Wordsworth	90
The Highwayman	Alfred Noyes	91
The Soldier	John Clare	97
The Shawl	W. Kean Seymour	97
Meeting at Night	Robert Browning	97
The Destruction of Sennacherib	Lord Byron	97
Parting at Morning	Robert Browning	100
Jaffàr	Leight Hunt	101
Still Waters	Anon.	102
Goliath	Walter de la Mare	102
From 'Sohrab and Rustum'	Matthew Arnold	104
How They Brought the Good News from Ghent to Aix	Robert Browning	106
Kubla Khan	S. T. Coleridge	109
After Blenheim	Robert Southey	110
The Rose	William Browne	113
From 'My Lost Youth'	H. W. Longfellow	114
The Death of Samson	John Milton	116
The Eastern Gate	Anon.	118
La Belle Dame Sans Merci	John Keats	119
The Cap and Bells	W. B. Yeats	121
The Galley of Count Arnaldos	H. W. Longfellow	123
A Lake and a Fairy Boat	Thomas Hood	124
The Mermaid	Alfred, Lord Tennyson	125
The Enchanted Island	L. A. Conolly	127
The Enchanted Shirt	John Hay	128
Bishop Hatto	Robert Southey	132
On a Certain Lady at Court	Alexander Pope	135
Get up and Bar the Door	Anon.	136
The Parrot: A True Story	Thomas Campbell	138

Introduction to The Teaching and Learning Notes and Guide	139
Teaching and Learning Notes and Guide	142
About the Editor	185
About Proverse Hong Kong / The Proverse Prize	187
Educational Books Published by Proverse	191

Part One

Poems to Speak

FUNERAL SONG

Whilst we sing the doleful knell
Of this princess' passing-bell,
Let the woods and valleys ring
Echoes to our sorrowing;
And the tenor of their song
Be ding-dong,
ding-dong, dong,
Ding, dong, dong,
Ding-dong.

Nature now shall boast no more
Of the riches of her store,
Since in this her chiefest prize
All the stock of beauty dies:
Then what cruel heart can long
Forbear to sing this sad ding-dong?
This sad ding-dong,
Ding-dong.

Fauns and sylvans of the woods,
Nymphs that haunt the crystal floods,
Savage beasts more milder than
The unrelenting hearts of men,
Be partakers of our moan,
And with us sing ding-dong, ding-dong,
Ding, dong, dong,
Ding-dong.

Anon.

A MORISCO

The sky is glad that stars above
Do give a brighter splendour:
The stars unfold their flaming gold,
To make the ground more tender:
The ground doth send a fragrant smell,
That air may be the sweeter:
The air doth charm the swelling seas
With pretty chirping metre:
The sea with river's water doth
Feed plants and flowers dainty:
The plants do yield their fruitful seed,
That beasts may live in plenty:
The beasts do give both food and cloth,
That men high Jove may honour;
And so the world runs merrily round,
When peace doth smile upon her.
Oh then, then oh: oh then, then oh:
This jubilee last for ever!
That foreign spite or civil fight,
Our quiet trouble never.

Jasper Fisher

ART THOU GONE IN HASTE?

Art thou gone in haste?
    I'll not forsake thee!
Runn'st thou ne'er so fast,
    I'll o'ertake thee!
O'er the dales or the downs,
    Through the green meadows,
From the fields, through the towns.
    To the dim shadows!

All along the plain,
    To the low fountains;
Up and down again,
    From the high mountains.
Echo, then, shall again
    Tell her I follow,
And the floods to the woods
    Carry my holla.
        Holla!
Ce! la! ho! ho! hu!

Elizabethan Lyric

THE BLACKSMITHS

Swart swarthy smiths besmattered with smoke
Drive me to death with din of their dints.
Such noise on nights heard no one never;
What knavish cry and clattering of knocks!
The snub nosed changelings cry after "col, col!"
And blow their bellows till all their brains burst:
"Huf, puf!" saith one; "haf paf!" another.
They spit and sprawl and spell many spells;
They grind teeth and gnash them, and groan together,
And hold them hot with their hard hammers.
Of bull's hide are their leather aprons.
Their shanks are shielded from the fierce sparks:
Heavy hammers they have; that are hard handled,
Stark strokes they strike on an anvil of steel
Lus, bus! Las, das! they strike in rotation
The Devil destroy such an awful noise.
The master lengthens a little piece, belabours a smaller,
Twines the two together, strikes a treble note
Tik, tak! Hie, hac! tiket, taket! tik, tak!
Lus, bus! las das! such lives they lead
All horseshoers: Christ give them sorrow
For none for these waterburners at night may rest.

Anon. (Modernised by Kenneth Sisam)

HUNTING SONG

The dusky Night rides down the Sky,
And ushers in the Morn;
The Hounds all join in glorious Cry
   The Huntsman winds his horn:
      And a Hunting we will go.

The Wife around her Husband throws
   Her Arms and begs his Stay;
"My Dear, it rains, and hails, and snows,
   You will not hunt to-day."
      But a Hunting we will go.

"A brushing Fox in yonder Wood,
   Secure to find we seek;
For why, I carried sound and good
   A cartload there last Week."
      And a Hunting we will go.

Away he goes, he flies the Rout,
    Their Steeds all spur and switch;
Some are thrown in, and some thrown out.
    And some thrown in the Ditch:
        But a Hunting we will go.

At length his Strength to Faintness worn,
    Poor Reynard ceases Flight;
Then hungry, homeward we return,
    To feast away the Night:
        Then a Drinking we will go.

Henry Fielding

MADRIGAL

Aye me, alas, heigh ho, heigh ho!
Thus doth Messalina go
Up and down the house a-crying,
For her monkey lies a-dying.
Death, thou art too cruel
To bereave her jewel,
Or to make a seizure
Of her only treasure.
If her monkey die,
She will sit and die,
She will sit and cry,
Fie fie fie fie fie!

Thomas Weekes

THE DEATH OF ADMIRAL BENBOW

Come all you sailors bold,
    Lend an ear,
Come all you sailors bold,
    Lend an ear:
'Tis of our Admiral's fame,
Brave Benbow called by name,
How he fought on the main
    You shall hear.

Brave Benbow he set sail
    For to fight,
Brave Benbow he set sail
    For to fight:
Brave Benbow he set sail,
With a fine and pleasant gale,
But his captains they turned tail
    In a fight.

Says Kirkby unto Wade,
    "I will run,"
Says Kirkby unto Wade,
    "I will run:
I value not disgrace,
Nor the losing of my place,
My foes I will not face
    With a gun."

'Twas the *Ruby* and *Noah's Ark*,
    Fought the French,
'Twas the *Ruby* and *Noah's Ark*,
    Fought the French:
And there was ten in all;
Poor souls they fought them all,
They recked them not at all,
    Nor their noise.

It was our Admiral's lot,
    With a chain-shot,
It was our Admiral's lot,
    With a chain-shot:
Our Admiral lost his legs,
And to his men he begs
"Fight on, my boys," he says,
    "'Tis my lot."

While the surgeon dressed his wounds,
    Thus he said,
While the surgeon dressed his wounds,
    Thus he said:
"Let my cradle now in haste
On the quarter deck be placed,
That the Frenchmen I may face,
    Till I'm dead."

And there bold Benbow lay,
    Crying out,
And there bold Benbow lay,
    Crying out:
"O let us tack once more,
We'll drive them to the shore,
As our fathers did before
    Long ago."

Anon.

SEA SHANTY

Away, haul away, boys, haul away together,
    Away, haul away, boys, haul away, O;
Away, haul away, boys, haul away together,
    Away, haul away, boys, haul away, O.

Louis was the King of France afore the Revoluti-on,
    Away, haul away, boys, haul away, O;
Louis was the King of France afore the Revoluti-on,
    Away, haul away, boys, haul away, O.

But Louis got his head cut off, which spoiled his
    con-stitu-ti-on,
    Away, haul away, boys, haul away, O;
But Louis got his head cut off, which spoiled his
    con-stitu-ti-on,
    Away, haul away, boys, haul away, O.

Traditional

OLD JOE IS DEAD AND GONE TO HELL

Old Joe is dead and gone to hell,
O we say so and we hope so;
Old Joe is dead, and gone to hell,
O poor old Joe.

The ship did sail, the winds did roar,
O we say so, and we hope so;
The ship did sail, the winds did roar,
O poor old Joe.

He's as dead as a nail in the lamp-room door,
O we say so and we hope so;
He's as dead as a nail in the lamp-room door,
O poor old Joe.

He won't come hazing us no more,
O we say so, and we hope so;
He won't come hazing us no more,
O poor old Joe.

Sea Shanty

ONE FRIDAY MORN

One Friday morn when we set sail,
    Not very far from land,
We there did espy a fair pretty maid
    With a comb and a glass in her hand, her hand, her hand,
With a comb and a glass in her hand.

    While the raging seas did roar,
    And the stormy winds did blow,
    While we jolly sailor boys were up into the top,
    And the land-lubbers lying down below, below,
      below,
    And the land-lubbers lying down below.

Then up starts the captain of our gallant ship,
    And a brave young man was he:
"I've a wife and child in fair Bristol town,
    But a widow I fear she will be."

    And the raging seas did roar,
    And the stormy winds did blow,
    While we jolly sailor boys were up into the top,
    And the land-lubbers lying down below, below,
      below,
    And the land-lubbers lying down below.

Then up starts the mate of our gallant ship,
    And a bold young man was he:
"Oh! I have a wife in fair Portsmouth town,
    But a widow I fear she will be."

    And the raging seas did roar,
    And the stormy winds did blow. *Etc.*

Then up starts the cook of our gallant ship,
    And a gruff old soul was he:
"Oh! but I have a wife in fair Plymouth town,
    But a widow I fear she will be."

    And the raging seas did roar,
    And the stormy winds did blow. *Etc.*

And then up spoke the little cabin-boy,
    And a pretty little boy was he;
"Oh! I am more grieved for my daddy and my mammy
    Than you for your wives all three."

    And the raging seas did roar,
    And the stormy winds did blow. *Etc.*

Then three times round went our gallant ship,
    And three times round went she;
And three times round went our gallant ship,
    And she sank to the bottom of the sea . . .

    And the raging seas did roar,
    And the stormy winds did blow.
    While we jolly sailor-boys were up into the top,
    And the land-lubbers lying down below, below,
        below,
    And the land-lubbers lying down below.

Old Shanty

TARANTELLA

Do you remember an Inn,
Miranda?
Do you remember an Inn?
And the tedding and the spreading
Of the straw for a bedding,
And the fleas that tease in the High Pyrenees,
And the wine that tasted of the tar?
And the cheers and the jeers of the young muleteers
(Under the vine of the dark verandah?)
Do you remember an Inn, Miranda,
Do you remember an Inn
And the cheers and the jeers of the young muleteers
Who hadn't got a penny,
And who weren't paying any,
And the hammer at the doors and the Din?
And the Hip! Hop! Hap!

Of the clap
Of the hands to the twirl and the swirl
Of the girl gone chancing,
Glancing,
Dancing,
Backing and Advancing,
Snapping of the clapper to the spin
Out and In—
And the Ting, Tong, Tang of the Guitar!
Do you remember an Inn,
Miranda?
Do you remember an Inn?

Never more;
Miranda,
Never more.
Only the high peaks hoar:
And Aragon a torrent at the door.
No sound
In the walls of the Halls where falls
The tread
Of the feet of the dead to the ground
No sound:
But the boom
Of the far Waterfall like Doom.

Hilaire Belloc

THE HIGH SONG
(*From* 'Requiem')

The high song is over. Silent is the lute now.
    They are crowned for ever and discrowned now.
Whether they triumphed or suffered they are mute now,
    Or at the most they are only a sound now.

The high song is over. There is none to complain now.
    No heart for healing, and none to break now.
They have gone, and they will not come again now.
    They are sleeping at last, and they will not wake now.

The high song is over. And we shall not mourn now.
    There was a thing to say, and it is said now.
It is as though all these had been unborn now,
    It is as though the world itself were dead now.

The high song is over. Even the echoes fail now;
    Winners and losers—they are only a theme now,
Their victory and defeat a half-forgotten tale now;
    And even the angels are only a dream now.

There is no need for blame, no cause for praise now.
    Nothing to hide, to change or to discover.
They were men and women. They have gone their ways now,
    As men and women must. The high song is over.

Humbert Wolfe

FULL FATHOM FIVE

Full fathom five thy father lies;
   Of his bones are coral made;
Those are pearls that were his eyes:
   Nothing of him that doth fade.
But doth suffer a sea-change
Into something rich and strange.
Sea-nymphs hourly ring his knell:
   Hark! now I hear them—
   Ding, dong, bell.

William Shakespeare

O MISTRESS MINE

O Mistress mine, where are you roaming?
O stay and hear; your true love's coming,
   That can sing both high and low:
Trip no further, pretty sweeting;
Journeys end in lovers meeting
   Every wise man's son doth know.

What is love? 'tis not hereafter;
Present mirth hath present laughter;
   What's to come is still unsure:
In delay there lies no plenty;
Then come kiss me, sweet and twenty,
   Youth's a stuff will not endure.

William Shakespeare

THE GYPSY LADDIE

It was late in the night when the Squire came home
Enquiring for his lady.
His servant made a sure reply:
She's gone with gipsum Davy.
    Rattle tum a gipsum gipsum
    Rattle tum a gipsum Davy.

O go catch up my milk-white steed,
The black one's not so speedy,
I'll ride all night till broad daylight,
Or overtake my lady.

He rode and he rode till he came to the town,
He rode till he came to Barley.
The tears came rolling down his cheeks,
And then he spied his lady.

It's come go back, my dearest dear,
Come go back, my honey;
It's come go back, my dearest dear,
And you never shall lack for money.

I won't go back my dearest dear.
I won't go back, my honey;
For I wouldn't give a kiss from gipsum's lips
For you and all your money.

It's go pull off those snow-white gloves,
A-made of Spanish leather,
And give to me your lily-white hand,
And bid farewell for ever.

It's she pulled off those snow-white gloves,
A-made of Spanish leather,
And gave to him her lily-white hand,
And bade farewell for ever.

She soon ran through her gay clothing,
Her velvet shoes and stockings;
Her gold ring off her finger's gone,
And the gold plate off her bosom.

O once I had a house and land,
Feather-bed and money;
But now I've come to an old straw pad,
With the gypsies dancing round me.

Folk Song

HIS GRANGE, OR PRIVATE WEALTH

Though Clock,
To tell how night draws hence, I've none,
A Cock,
I have, to sing how day draws on.
I have
A maid (my Prew) by good luck sent,
To save
That little, Fates me gave or lent.
A Hen
I keep, which creeking day by day,
Tells when
She goes her long white egg to lay.
A Goose
I have, which, with a jealous ear,
Lets loose
Her tongue, to tell what danger's near.
A Lamb
I keep (tame) with my morsels fed,
Whose Dam
An orphan left him (lately dead).
A Cat
I keep, that plays about my House,
Grown fat,
With eating many a miching Mouse.
To these
A Trasy I do keep, whereby
I please
The more my rural privacy:
Which are
But toys, to give my heart some ease;
Where care
None is, slight things do lightly please.

Robert Herrick

THE GARDEN SEAT

Its former green is blue and thin,
And its once firm legs sink in and in;
Soon it will break down unaware,
Soon it will break down unaware.

At night when reddest flowers are black
Those who once sat thereon come back;
Quite a row of them sitting there,
Quite a row of them sitting there.

With them the seat does not break down,
Nor the winter freeze them, nor floods drown,
For they are as light as upper air,
They are as light as upper air!

Thomas Hardy

THE BELL-MAN

From noise of Scare-fires rest ye free,
From Murders—Benedicite.
From all mischances that may fright
Your pleasing slumbers in the night:
Mercie secure ye all, and keep
The Goblin from ye, while ye sleep.
Past one o'clock, and almost two.
My Masters all, Good day to you!

Robert Herrick

POOR OLD HORSE

My clothing was once of the linsey woolsey fine,
My tail it grew at length, my coat did likewise shine;
But now I'm growing old; my beauty does decay,
My master frowns upon me; one day I heard him say,
Poor old horse; poor old horse.

Once I was kept in the stable snug and warm,
To keep my tender limbs from any cold or harm;
But now, in open fields, I am forced to go,
In all sorts of weather, let it be hail, rain, freeze, or snow.
Poor old horse; poor old horse.

Once I was fed on the very best corn and hay
That ever grew in yon fields, or in yon meadows gay;
But now there's no such doing can I find at all,
I'm glad to pick the green sprouts that grow behind yon wall.
Poor old horse; poor old horse.

"You are old, you are cold, you are deaf, dull, dumb and slow,
You are not fit for anything, or in my team to draw.
You have eaten all my hay, you have spoiled all my straw,
So hang him, whip, stick him, to the huntsman let him go."
Poor old horse; poor old horse.

My hide unto the tanners then I would freely give,
My body to the hound dogs, I would rather die than live,
Likewise my poor old bones that have carried you many a mile,
Over hedges, ditches, brooks, bridges, likewise gates and stiles.
Poor old horse; poor old horse.

Anon.

SONG FROM THE SHIP
(From *Death's Jest-Book*)

To sea, to sea! The calm is o'er;
The wanton water leaps in sport,
And rattles down the pebbly shore;
The dolphin wheels, the sea-cows snort,
And unseen Mermaids' pearly song
Comes bubbling up, the weeds among.
    Fling broad the sail, dip deep the oar;
    To sea, to sea! The calm is o'er.

To sea, to sea! our wide-winged bark
Shall billowy cleave its sunny way,
And with its shadow, fleet and dark,
Break the caved Tritons' azure day,
Like mighty eagle soaring light
O'er antelopes on Alpine height.
    The anchor heaves, the ship swings free,
    The sails swell full. To sea, to sea!

T. L. Beddoes

SONG

To all you ladies now at land
    We men at sea indite;
But first would have you understand
    How hard it is to write:
The Muses now, and Neptune too,
We must implore to write to you—
    With a fa, la, la, la, la.

For though the Muses should prove kind,
    And fill our empty brain,
Yet if rough Neptune rouse the wind
    To wave the azure main,
Our paper, pen, and ink, and we,
Roll up and down our ships at sea—
    With a fa, la, la, la, la.

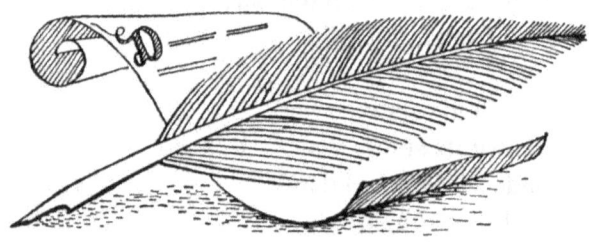

Then if we write not by each post,
    Think not we are unkind;
Nor yet conclude our ships are lost
    By Dutchmen or by wind:
Our tears we'll send a speedier way,
The tide shall bring them twice a day—
    With a fa, la, la, la, la.

The King with wonder and surprise
    Will swear the seas grow bold,
Because the tides will higher rise
    Than e'er they did of old:
But let him know it is our tears
Bring floods of grief to Whitehall stairs—
    With a fa, la, la, la, la.

But now our fears tempestuous grow
    And cast our hopes away;
Whilst you, regardless of our woe,
    Sit careless at a play:
Perhaps permit some happier man
To kiss your hand, or flirt your fan—
    With a fa, la, la, la, la.

When any mournful tune you hear,
    That dies in every note
As if it sigh'd with each man's care
    For being so remote,
Think then how often love we've made
To you, when all those tunes were play'd—
    With a fa, la, la, la, la.

In justice you can not refuse
    To think of our distress,
When we for hopes of honour lose
    Our certain happiness:
All those designs are but to prove
Ourselves more worthy of your love—
    With a fa, la, la, la, la.

And now we've told you all our loves.
    And likewise all our fears,
In hopes this declaration moves
    Some pity for our tears:
Let's hear of no inconstancy—
We have too much of that at sea—
    With a fa, la, la, la, la.

Charles Sackville, Earl of Dorset

THE MAID OF THE MOOR

Maiden in the moor lay,
   In the moor lay,
Seven nights full, seven nights full,
Maiden in the moor lay,
   In the moor lay,
Seven nights full and a day.

Well was her meat;
   What was her meat?
   The primrose and the—
   The primrose and the—
Well was her meat;
What was her meat?
   The primrose and the violet.

Well was her drink;
   What was her drink?
   The cold water of—
   The cold water of—
Well was her drink;
What was her drink?
   The cold water of the well-spring.

Well was her bower;
    What was her bower?
    The red rose and the—
    The red rose and the—
Well was her bower;
What was her bower?
    The red rose and the lily flower.

Anon. (Modernised by Kenneth Sisam)

THE HAPPY HEART

Art thou poor, yet hast thou golden slumbers?
    O sweet content!
Art thou rich, yet is thy mind perplexed?
    O punishment!
Dost thou laugh to see how fools are vexed
To add to golden numbers, golden numbers?
O sweet content! O sweet, O sweet content!
    Work apace, apace, apace, apace;
    Honest labour bears a lovely face;
Then hey nonny, nonny, hey nonny nonny!

Canst drink the waters of the crisped spring?
    O sweet content!
Swimm'st thou in wealth, yet sink'st in thine own tears?
    O punishment!
Then he that patiently want's burden bears
No burden bears, but is a king, a king!
O sweet content! O sweet, O sweet content!
    O work apace, apace, apace, apace;
    Honest labour bears a lovely face;
Then hey nonny nonny, hey nonny nonny!

Thomas Dekker

ALL FOR LOVE

O talk not to me of a name great in story;
The days of our youth are the days of our glory;
And the myrtle and ivy of sweet two-and-twenty
Are worth all your laurels though ever so plenty.

What are garlands and crowns to the brow that is wrinkled?
'Tis but as a dead flower with May-dew besprinkled.
Then away with all such from the head that is hoary—
What care I for wreaths that can only give glory?

O Fame!—If I e'er took delight in thy praises,
'Twas less for the sake of thy high-sounding phrases,
Than to see the bright eyes of the dear one discover
She thought that I was not unworthy to love her.

There chiefly I sought thee, there only I found thee;
Her glance was the best of the rays that surround thee;
When it sparkled o'er aught that was bright in my story,
I knew it was love and I felt it was glory.

Lord Byron

THE BELLS OF SHANDON

With deep affection,
And recollection,
I often think of
   Those Shandon bells,
Whose sounds so wild would,
In the days of childhood,
Fling around my cradle
   Their magic spells.

On this I ponder
Where'er I wander,
And thus grow fonder,
    Sweet Cork of thee;
With thy bells of Shandon,
That sound so grand on
The pleasant waters
    Of the River Lee.

I've heard bells chiming
Full many a clime in.
Tolling sublime in
    Cathedral shrine,
While at a glib rate
Brass tongues would vibrate—
But all their music
    Spoke naught like thine;

For memory, dwelling
On each proud swelling
Of the belfry knelling
    Its bold notes free,
Made the bells of Shandon
Sound far more grand on
The pleasant waters
    Of the River Lee.

I've heard bells tolling
Old Adrian's Mole in
Their thunder rolling
    From the Vatican,
And cymbals glorious
Swinging uproarious
In the gorgeous turrets
    Of Notre Dame;

But their sounds were sweeter
Than the dome of Peter
Flings o'er the Tiber,
   Pealing solemnly—
O, the bells of Shandon
Sound far more grand on
The pleasant waters
Of the River Lee.

There's a bell in Moscow,
While on tower and kiosk O!
In Saint Sophia
   The Turkman gets,
And loud in air
Calls men to prayer
From the tapering summits
   Of tall minarets.

Such empty phantom
I freely grant them;
But there's an anthem
   More dear to me,—
'Tis the bells of Shandon,
That sound so grand on
The pleasant waters
   Of the River Lee.

Francis Mahoney

THE THREE WISE MEN OF GOTHAM

Seamen three! What men be ye?
Gotham's three wise men we be.
Whither in your bowl so free?
To take the moon from out the sea.
The bowl goes trim. The moon doth shine.
And your ballast is old wine.
And your ballast is old wine.

Who are thou, so fast adrift?
I am he they call Old Care.
Here on board we will thee lift.
No: I may not enter there.
Wherefore so? 'Tis Jove's decree.
In a bowl Care may not be.
In a bowl Care may not be.

Fear ye not the waves that roll?
No: in charmed bowl we swim.
What the charm that floats the bowl?
Water may not pass the brim.
The bowl goes trim. The moon doth shine.
And your ballast is old wine.
And your ballast is old wine.

T. L. Peacock

ODE

We are the music-makers,
    And we are the dreamers of dreams,
Wandering by the lone sea-breakers,
    And sitting by desolate streams;
World-losers and world-forsakers,
    On whom the pale moon gleams:
Yet we are the movers and shakers
    Of the world for ever, it seems.

With wonderful deathless ditties
    We build up the world's great cities,
And out of the fabulous story
    We fashion an empire's glory:
One man with a dream, at pleasure,
    Shall go forth and conquer a crown;
And three with a new song's measure
    Can trample an empire down.

We, in the ages lying
    In the buried past of the earth,
Built Nineveh with our sighing
    And Babel itself with our mirth:
And o'erthrew them with prophesying
    To the old of the new world's worth;
For each age is a dream that is dying,
    Or one that is coming to birth.

Arthur O'Shaughnessy

MARCHING ALONG

Kentish Sir Byng stood for his King,
Bidding the crop-headed Parliament swing:
And, pressing a troop unable to stoop
And see the rogues flourish and honest folk droop,
Marched them along, fifty score strong
Great-hearted gentlemen, singing this song.
Marching along, fifty-score strong,
Great-hearted gentlemen singing this song.
God for King Charles! Pym and such carles
To the Devil that prompts 'em their treasonous parles!
Cavaliers, up! Lips from the cup,
Hands from the pasty, nor bite take nor sup
Till you're—
Marching along, fifty-score strong,
Great-hearted gentlemen, singing this song.
Hampden to hell, and his obsequies knell
Serve Hazelrig, Fiennes, and young Harry as well!
England good cheer! Rupert is near!
Kentish and loyalists, keep we not here
Marching along, fifty-score strong,
Great-hearted gentlemen singing this song!
Then, God for King Charles! Pym and his snarls
To the Devil that pricks on such pestilent carles!
Hold by the right, you double your might; So, onward to
Nottingham, fresh for the fight,
March we along, fifty-score strong,
Great-hearted gentlemen, singing this song!

Robert Browning

SONG OF THE BOWMEN OF SHU
(From the Chinese of Bunno, 1100 B.C.)

Here we are, picking the first fern-shoots
And saying: When shall we get back to our country?
Here we are because we have the Ken-nin for our foemen,
We have no comfort because of these Mongols.
We grub the first fern-shoots,
When anyone says "Return", the others are full of sorrow.
Sorrowful minds, sorrow is strong, we are hungry and
 thirsty.
Our defence is not yet made sure, no one can let his friend
 return.
We grub the old fern-stalks.
We say: Will we be let to go back in October?
There is no ease in royal affairs, we have no comfort.
Our sorrow is bitter, but we would not return to our
 country.

What flower has come into blossom?
Whose chariot? The General's.
Horses, his horses even, are tired. They were strong.
We have no rest, three battles a month.
By heaven, his horses are tired.
The generals are on them, the soldiers are by them.
The horses are well trained, the generals have ivory arrows
and quivers ornamented with fish-skin.
The enemy is swift, we must be careful.
When we set out, the willows were drooping with spring,
We come back in the snow,
We go slowly, we are hungry and thirsty,
Our mind is full of sorrow, who will know of our grief?

Ezra Pound

AN INDIAN SUMMER ON THE PRAIRIE

In the Beginning
The sun is a huntress young,
The sun is a red, red joy,
The sun is an Indian girl,
Of the tribe of the Illinois.

Mid-morning
The sun is a smouldering fire,
That creeps through the high grey plain,
And leaves not a bush of cloud
To blossom with flowers of rain.

Noon
The sun is a wounded deer,
That treads pale grass in the skies,
Shaking his golden horns,
Flashing his baleful eyes.

Sunset
The sun is an eagle old.
There in the windless west,
Atop of the spirit-cliffs
He builds him a crimson nest,

Vachel Lindsay

Part Two

Pictures in Poetry

JAQUES' SEVEN AGES OF MAN

All the world's a stage,
And all the men and women merely players:
They have their exits and their entrances;
And one man in his time plays many parts,
His acts being seven ages. At first the infant,
Mewling and puking in the nurse's arms.
And then the whining school-boy, with his satchel
And shining morning face, creeping like snail
Unwillingly to school. And then the lover,
Sighing like furnace, with a woeful ballad
Made to his mistress' eyebrow. Then a soldier,
Full of strange oaths, and bearded like the pard,
Jealous in honour, sudden and quick in quarrel,
Seeking the bubble reputation
Even in the cannon's mouth. And then the justice,
In fair round belly with good capon lined,
With eyes severe and beard of formal cut,
Full of wise saws and modern instances;
And so he plays his part. The sixth age shifts
Into the lean and slippered pantaloon,
With spectacles on nose and pouch on side,
His youthful hose well sav'd, a world too wide
For his shrunk shank; and his big manly voice,
Turning again toward childish treble, pipes
And whistles in his sound. Last scene of all,
That ends this strange eventful history,
Is second childishness and mere oblivion,
Sans teeth, sans eyes, sans taste, sans everything.

William Shakespeare (From *As You Like It*)

BREAK, BREAK, BREAK

Break, break, break,
   On thy cold grey stones, O Sea!
And I would that my tongue could utter
   The thoughts that arise in me.

O well for the fisherman's boy,
   That he shouts with his sister at play!
O well for the sailor lad,
   That he sings in his boat on the bay!

And the stately ships go on
   To their haven under the hill;
But O for the touch of a vanish'd hand,
   And the sound of a voice that is still!

Break, break, break,
   At the foot of thy crags, O Sea!
But the tender grace of a day that is dead
   Will never come back to me.

Alfred, Lord Tennyson

TROPIC RAIN

As the single pang of the blow, when the metal is mingled well,
Rings and lives and resounds in all the bounds of the bell,
So the thunder above spoke with a single tongue,
So in the heart of the mountain the sound of it rumbled and clung.

Sudden the thunder was drowned—quenched was the levin light—
And the angel-spirit of rain laughed out loud in the night.
Loud as the maddened river raves in the cloven glen,
Angel of rain! you laughed and leaped on the roofs of men;
And the sleepers sprang in their beds, and joyed and feared as you fell.
You struck, and my cabin quailed; the roof of it roared like a bell.

You spoke, and at once the mountain shouted and shook with brooks.
You ceased, and the day returned, rosy, with virgin looks.
And methought that beauty and terror are only one, not two;
And the world has room for love, and death, and thunder, and dew;
And all the sinews of hell slumber in summer air;
And the face of God is a rock, but the face of the rock is fair.
Beneficent streams of tears flow at the finger of pain;
And out of the cloud that smites, beneficent rivers of rain.

Robert Louis Stevenson

OZYMANDIAS

I met a traveller from an antique land
Who said: Two vast and trunkless legs of stone
Stand in the desert. Near them, on the sand,
Half sunk, a shatter'd visage lies, whose frown,
And wrinkled lip, and sneer of cold command,
Tell that its sculptor well those passions read
Which yet survive, stamp'd on these lifeless things,
The hand that mock'd them and the heart that fed;
And on the pedestal these words appear:
"My name is Ozymandias, King of kings:
Look on my works, ye Mighty, and despair!"
Nothing beside remains. Round the decay
Of that colossal wreck, boundless and bare
The lone and level lands stretch far away.

P. B. Shelley

THE ICE-CART

Perched on my city office-stool
I watched with envy, while a cool
And lucky carter handled ice ...
And I was wandering in a trice,
Far from the grey and grimy heat
Of that intolerable street,
O'er sapphire berg and emerald floe,
Beneath the still, cold ruby glow
Of everlasting Polar night.
Bewildered by the queer half-light,
Until I stumbled, unawares,
Upon a creek where big white bears
Plunged headlong down with flourished heels,
And floundered after shining seals
Through shivering seas of blinding blue.

And as I watched them, ere I knew,
I'd stripped, and I was swimming, too,
Among the seal-pack, young and hale,
And thrusting on with threshing tail,
With twist and twirl and sudden leap
Through crackling ice and salty deep—
Diving and doubling with my kind,
Until, at last, we left behind
Those big white blundering bulks of death,
And lay, at length, with panting breath
Upon a far untravelled floe,
Beneath a gentle drift of snow—
Snow drifting gently, fine and white,
Out of the endless Polar night,
Falling and falling evermore
Upon that far untravelled shore,
Till I was buried fathoms deep
Beneath that cold, white drifting sleep—
Sleep drifting deep,
Deep drifting sleep . . .

The carter cracked a sudden whip;
I clutched my stool with startled grip,
Awakening to the grimy heat
Of that intolerable street.

W. W. *Gibson*

THE LISTENERS

"Is there anybody there?" said the Traveller,
    Knocking on the moonlit door;
And his horse in the silence champed the grasses
    Of the forest's ferny floor:
And a bird flew up out of the turret,
    Above the Traveller's head:
And he smote upon the door again a second time;
    "Is there anybody there?" he said.
But no one descended to the Traveller;
    No head from the leaf-fringed sill
Leaned over and looked into his grey eyes,
    Where he stood perplexed and still.
But only a host of phantom listeners
    That dwelt in the lone house then
Stood listening in the moonlight
    To that voice from the world of men:
Stood thronging the faint moonbeams on the dark stair,
    That goes down to the empty hall,
Hearkening in an air stirred and shaken
    By the lonely Traveller's call.
And he felt in his heart their strangeness,
    Their stillness answering his cry,
While his horse moved, cropping the dark turf,
    'Neath the starred and leafy sky;
For he suddenly smote on the door, even
    Louder, and lifted his head:
"Tell them I came, and no one answered,

    That I kept my word," he said.
Never made the least stir the listeners,
    Though every word he spake
Fell echoing through the shadowiness of the still house
    From the one man left awake:
Ay, they heard his foot upon the stirrup,
    And the sound of iron on stone,
And how the silence surged softly backward,
    When the plunging hoofs were gone.

Walter De La Mare

ON FIRST LOOKING INTO CHAPMAN'S 'HOMER'

Much have I travell'd in the realms of gold,
    And many goodly states and kingdoms seen;
    Round many western islands have I been
Which bards in fealty to Apollo hold.
Oft of one wide expanse had I been told
    That deep-browed Homer ruled as his demesne;
    Yet did I never breathe its pure serene
Till I heard Chapman speak out loud and bold:
Then felt I like some watcher of the skies
    When a new planet swims into his ken;
Or like stout Cortez when with eagle eyes
    He star'd at the Pacific—and all his men
Look'd at each other with a wild surmise—
    Silent, upon a peak in Darien.

John Keats

DOCKS

When paint or steel or wood are wearing thin,
Then they come in:
The liners, schooners, merchantmen, and tramps,
Upon a head of water pressing hard
On gates of greenheart wood, that close and guard
The docks, till lintels, clamps,
Swing suddenly on quoins steel-pivoted,
With harsh complaint and clang,
And then above the walls arise and spread
Top-gallant yards or funnel, spanker-vang
Or dolphin-striker; figure-heads arise
That settling sway
Beside an inn; a mermaid's breasts and eyes
Beneath a bowsprit glare beside a dray.
All docks are wonderful, whether beside
The estuaries or foreshores robbed of sea,
Where jetties and much dredging keep them free,
And the strong constant scouring of the tide
Sweeps down the silt; or where by sandy dune

The neap-tides leave them dry, or flood tides dash
With a vindictive lash
At the conjunction of the sun and moon.
And wonderful are dry docks, where the ships
Are run on keel-props held by timber-shores,
And sterns and prores
Stand up for scraper's work, and the paint drips
Among algae and mussels; wonderful when
Docks still are in the building, and the pumps
Move water from the sumps,
And derricks, little trains, and shouting men
Dump clustered cylinders upon the gravel,
And through the sky large blocks of granite travel,
Dangling to place to make the sills. Or when
As now by Thames the running currents flush
The sluices of the locks, and seek to rush
Reverse-gate strengthening the entrances,
Harry the boats, and shift
The refuse of the town and littoral drift;
And in the dusk the slums are palaces.
They wait upon the sea.
And wharf and jetty, stately in the grime
Make commerce classical, and turn sublime
The warehouse crammed with jute or flax or tea.

Dorothy Wellesley

SONG OF THREE GORGES

From the twelve Hills of the Witches I see the Nine Peaks
 rise;
Beyond my prows a myriad tints flush autumn's empty
 skies.
Untrue the legend, "Morning clouds, and evening rain,"
The howling of gibbons in bright moonlight fills the plain.
When long June days begin
I wander to Nan-pin,
And moor my boat to a little quay
Where monkeys swing from tree to tree.
Now shadows gloom Ch'u Yuan's grey memorial;
And by the tomb of Yu red roses fall.

LuYu

FRAGMENT

The cataract, whirling to the precipice,
 Elbows down rocks and, shouldering, thunders through.
Roars, howls, and stifled murmurs never cease;
 Hell and its agonies seem hid below.
Thick rolls the mist, that smokes and falls in dew;
 The trees and greenwood wear the deepest green.
Horrible mysteries in the gulf stare through,
 Roars of a million tongues, and none knows what they
  mean.

John Clare

THE LYCHEE

Fruit white and lustrous as a pearl—
Lambent as the jewel of Ho, more strange
Than the saffron-stone of Hsia.
Now sigh we at the beauty of its show,
Now triumph in its taste.
Sweet juices lie in the mouth,
Soft scents invade the mind.
All flavours here are joined, yet none is master;
A hundred diverse tastes
Blend in such harmony no man can say
That one outstrips the rest. Sovereign of sweets,
Peerless, pre-eminent fruit, who dwellest apart
In noble solitude!

Wang I (Translated from the Chinese by Arthur Waley)

THE MUSIC OF THE SEA

Now, lay thine ear against this golden sand,
    And thou shalt hear the music of the sea,
Those hollow tones it plays against the land—
Is't not a rich and wondrous melody?
I have lain hours, and fancied in its tone
I heard the language of ages gone.

Thomas Hood

THE KINGFISHER

It was the Rainbow gave thee birth,
    And left thee all her lovely hues;
And, as her mother's name was Tears,
    So runs it in thy blood to choose
For haunts the lonely pools, and keep
In company with trees that weep.

Go you and, with such glorious hues,
    Live with proud peacocks in green parks;
On lawns as smooth as shining glass,
    Let every feather show its marks;
Get thee on boughs and clap thy wings
Before the windows of proud kings.

Nay, lovely Bird, thou art not vain;
    Thou hast no proud ambitious mind;
I also love a quiet place
    That's green, away from all mankind;
A lonely pool, and let a tree
Sigh with her bosom over me.

W. H. Davies

THE VILLAGE SCHOOLMASTER
(*From* 'The Deserted Village')

Beside yon straggling fence that skirts the way,
With blossomed furze unprofitably gay,
There, in his noisy mansion, skilled to rule
The village master taught his little school;
A man severe he was, and stern to view;
I knew him very well, and every truant knew;
Well had the boding tremblers learned to trace
The day's disasters in his morning face;
Full well they laughed with counterfeited glee
At all his jokes, for many a joke had he;
Full well the busy whisper, circling round,
Conveyed the dismal tidings when he frowned.
Yet he was kind; or if severe in aught,
The love he bore to learning was in fault.
The village all declared how much he knew;
'Twas certain he could write and cypher too;
Lands he could measure, terms and tides presage,
And even the story ran that he could gauge.
In arguing too, the parson owned his skill,
For e'en though vanquished, he could argue still;
While words of learned length and thund'ring sound
Amazed the gazing rustics ranged around,
And still they gazed, and still the wonder grew
That one small head could carry all he knew.
But past is all his fame. The very spot,
Where many a time he triumphed, is forgot.

Oliver Goldsmith

THE KITTEN AND THE FALLING LEAVES

See the kitten on the wall,
Sporting with the leaves that fall,
Withered leaves—one—two—and three—
From the lofty elder tree!
Through the calm and frosty air
Of this morning bright and fair,
Eddying round and round they sink
Softly, slowly: one might think
From the motions that are made
Every little leaf conveyed
Sylph or Fairy hither tending
To this lower world descending,
Each invisible and mute,
In his wavering parachute.

But the Kitten, how she starts,
Crouches, stretches, paws and darts!
First at one, and then its fellow,
Just as light and just as yellow;
There are many now—now one—
Now they stop and there are none.
What intenseness of desire
In her upward eye of fire,
With a tiger-leap half-way
Now she meets the coming prey,
Lets it go as fast, and then
Has it in her power again:

Now she works with three or four,
Like an Indian conjuror;
Quick as he in feats of art,
Far beyond in joy of heart.
Were her antics played in the eye
Of a thousand standers-by,
Clapping hands with shout and stare,

What would little Tabby care
For the plaudits of the crowd?
Over happy to be proud,
Over wealthy in the treasure
Of her own exceeding pleasure!

William Wordsworth

I STOOD TIPTOE

I stood tiptoe upon a little hill,
The air was cooling, and so very still,
That the sweet buds, which with a modest pride
Pull droopingly, in slanting curve aside,
Their scanty-leaved and finely-tapering stems,
Had not yet lost their starry diadems
Caught from the early sobbing of the morn.
The clouds were pure and white as flocks new shorn,
And fresh from the clear brook; sweetly they slept
On the blue fields of heaven, and then there crept
A little noiseless noise among the leaves,
Born of the very sigh that silence leaves;
For not the faintest motion could be seen
Of all the shades that slanted o'er the green.

John Keats

From PIPPA PASSES

Day!
Faster and more fast,
O'er night's brim, day boils at last:
Boils, pure gold, o'er the cloud-cup's brim
Where spurting and suppressed it lay,
For not a froth-flake touched the rim
Of yonder gap in the solid gray
Of the eastern cloud, an hour away;
But forth one wavelet, then another, curled,
Till the whole sunrise, not to be suppressed,
Rose, reddened, and its seething breast
Flickered in bounds, grew gold, then overflowed the world.

Robert Browning

HELEN'S TOWER

Helen's Tower, here I stand,
Dominant over sea and land.
Son's love built me, and I hold
Mother's love in letter'd gold.
Love is in and out of time,
I am mortal stone and lime.
Would my granite girth were strong
As either love, to last as long!
I should wear my crown entire
To and thro' the Doomsday fire,
And be found of angel eyes
In earth's recurring Paradise.

Alfred, Lord Tennyson

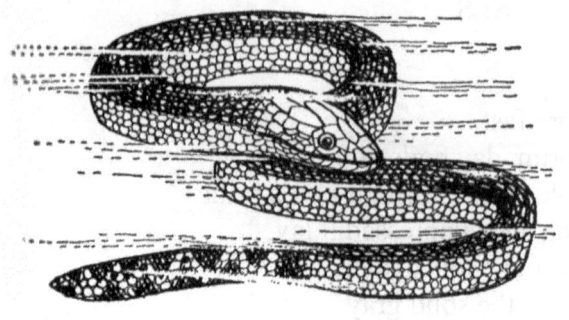

From THE RIME OF THE ANCIENT MARINER

Beyond the shadow of the ship,
I watched the water-snakes:
They moved in tracks of shining white,
And when they reared, the elfish light
Fell off in hoary flakes.

Within the shadow of the ship
I watched their rich attire:
Blue, glossy green and velvet black,
They coiled and swam; and every track
Was a flash of golden fire.

O happy living things! no tongue
Their beauty might declare:
A spring of love gushed from my heart,
And I blessed them unaware!
Sure my kind saint took pity on me,
And I blessed them unaware.

S. T. Coleridge

THE BULL
(*From* THE SEASONS)

Through all his lusty veins
The bull, deep-scorched, the raging passion feels.
Of pasture sick, and negligent of food,
Scarce seen he wades among the yellow broom,
While o'er his ample sides the rambling sprays
Luxuriant shoot; or through the mazy wood
Dejected wanders, nor the enticing bud
Crops, though it presses on his careless sense.
And oft, in jealous maddening fancy wrapt,
He seeks the fight; and idly butting, feigns
His rival gored in every knotty trunk.
Him should he meet, the bellowing war begins:
Their eyes flash fury; to the hollowed earth,
Whence the sand flies, they mutter bloody deeds,
And, groaning deep, the impetuous battle mix:
While the fair heifer, balmy-breathing near,
Stands kindling up their rage. The trembling steed,
With this hot impulse seized in every nerve,
Nor heeds the rein, nor hears the sounding throng;

Blows are not felt; but, tossing high his head,
And by the well-known joy to distant plains
Attracted strong, all wild he bursts away;
O'er rocks, and woods, and craggy mountains flies;
And, neighing, on the aerial summit takes
The exciting gale; then, steep-descending cleaves
The headlong torrents foaming down the hills,
Even where the madness of the straitened stream
Turns in black eddies round: such is the force
With which his frantic heart and sinews swell.

James Thomson

ON THE SEA

It keeps eternal whisperings around
Desolate shores, and with its mighty swell
Gluts twice ten thousand caverns, till the spell
Of Hecate leaves them their old shadowy sound.
Often 'tis in such gentle temper found,
That scarcely will the very smallest shell
Be mov'd for days from where it sometime fell,
When last the winds of heaven were unbound.
Oh ye! who have your eye-balls vex'd and tir'd,
Feast them upon the wideness of the sea;
Oh ye! whose ears are dinned with uproar rude,
Or fed too much with cloying melody—
Sit ye near some old cavern's mouth, and brood
Until ye start, as if the sea-nymphs quir'd!

John Keats

THE BELFRY

Dark is the stair, and humid the old walls
Wherein it winds, on worn stones, up the tower.
Only by loophole chinks at intervals
Pierces the late glow of this August hour.

Two truant children climb the stairway dark,
With joined hands, half in glee and half in fear,
The boy mounts brisk, the girl hangs back to hark
If the gruff sexton their light footsteps hear.

Dazzled at last they gain the belfry-room.
Barred rays through shutters hover across the floor
Dancing in dust; so fresh they come from gloom
That breathless they pause wondering at the door.

How hushed it is! what smell of timbers old
From cobwebbed beams! The warm light here and there
Edging in darkness, sleeps in pools of gold,
Or weaves fantastic shadows through the air.

How motionless the huge bell! Straight and stiff,
Ropes through the floor rise to the rafters dim.
The shadowy round of metal hangs, as if
No force could ever lift its gleamy rim.

A child's awe, a child's wonder, who shall trace
What dumb thoughts on its waxen softness write
In such a spell-brimmed, time-forgotten place,
Bright in that strangeness of approaching night?

As these two gaze, their fingers tighter press;
For suddenly the slow bell upward heaves
Its vast mouth, the cords quiver at the stress,
And ere the heart prepare, the ear receives

Full on its delicate sense the plangent stroke
Of violent, iron, reverberating sound.
As if the tower in all its stones awoke,
Deep echoes tremble, again in clangour drowned,

That starts without a whirr of frighted wings
And holds these young hearts shaken, hushed, and thrilled,
Like frail reeds in a rushing stream, like strings
Of music, or like trees with tempest filled,

And rolls in wide waves out o'er the lone land,
Tone following tone toward the far-setting sun,
Till where in fields long shadowed reapers stand
Bowed heads look up, and lo, the day is done . . .

Laurence Binyon

HORSES ON THE CAMARGUE

In the grey wastes of dread,
The haunts of shattered gulls where nothing moves
But in a shroud of silence like the dead,
I heard a sudden harmony of hooves,
And, turning, saw afar
A hundred snowy horses unconfined,
The silver runaways of Neptune's car
Racing, spray-curled, like waves before the wind.
Sons of the Mistral, fleet
As him with whose strong gusts they love to flee,
Who shod the flying thunders on their feet
And plumed them with the snortings of the sea;
Theirs is no earthly breed
Who only haunt the verges of the earth
And only on the sea's salt herbage feed—
Surely the great white breakers gave them birth.

For when for years a slave,
A horse of the Camargue, in alien lands,
Should catch some far-off fragrance of the wave
Carried far inland from his native sands,
Many have told the tale
Of how in fury, foaming at the rein,
He hurls his rider; and with lifted tail,
With coal-red eyes and cataracting mane,
Heading his course for home,
Though sixty foreign leagues before him sweep,
Will never rest until he breathes the foam
And hears the native thunder of the deep.
But when the great gusts rise
And lash their anger on these arid coasts,
When the scared gulls career with mournful cries
And whirl across the waste like driven ghosts:
When hail and fire converge,
The only souls to which they strike no pain
Are the white-crested fillies of the surge
And the white horses of the windy plain.
Then in their strength and pride
The stallions of the wilderness rejoice;
They feel their Master's trident in their side
And high and shrill they answer to his voice.

With white tails smoking free,
Long streaming manes and arching necks, they show
Their kinship to their sisters of the sea—
And forward hurl their thunderbolts of snow.
Still out of hardship bred,
Spirits of such power and beauty and delight
Have ever on such frugal pastures fed
And loved to course with tempests through the night.

Roy Campbell

SHE WALKS IN BEAUTY

She walks in beauty, like the night
    Of cloudless climes and starry skies;
And all that's best of dark and bright
    Meet in her aspect and her eyes:
Thus mellow'd to that tender Light
    Which heaven to gaudy day denies.

One shade the more, one ray the less,
    Had half impair'd the nameless grace
Which waves in every raven tress,
    Or softly lightens o'er her face;
Where thoughts serenely sweet express
    How pure, how dear their dwelling-place.

And on that cheek, and o'er that brow,
    So soft, so calm, yet eloquent,
The smiles that win, the tints that glow,
    But tell of days in goodness spent,
A mind at peace with all below,
    A heart whose love is innocent!

Lord Byron

THE KRAKEN

Below the thunders of the upper deep;
Far, far beneath in the abysmal sea,
His ancient, dreamless, uninvaded sleep
The Kraken sleepeth; faintest sunlights flee
About his shadowy sides: above him swell
Huge sponges of millennial growth and height;
And far away into the sickly light,
From many a wondrous grot and secret cell
Unnumber'd and enormous polypi
Winnow with giant fins the slumbering green.
There hath he lain for ages and will lie
Battening upon huge seaworms in his sleep,
Until the latter fire shall heat the deep;
Then once by men and angels to be seen,
In roaring he shall rise and on the surface die.

Alfred, Lord Tennyson

A FEAST OF LANTERNS

    In spring for sheer delight
I set the lanterns swinging through the trees,
    Bright as the myriad argosies of night,
    That ride the clouded billows of the sky.
Red dragons leap and plunge in gold and silver seas.
    And, O my garden gleaming cold and white,
    Thou hast outshone the far faint moon on high.

Yuan Mei

THE NILE

It flows through old hushed Egypt and its sands,
    Like some grave mighty thought threading a dream,
    And times and things, as in that vision, seem
Keeping along it their eternal stands—
Caves, pillars, pyramids, the shepherd bands
    That roamed through the young world, the glory extreme
    Of high Sesostris, and that southern beam,
The laughing queen that caught the world's great hands.
Then comes a mightier silence, stern and strong,
As of a world left empty of its throng,
And the void weighs on us; and then we wake,
And hear the fruitful stream lapsing along
    'Twixt villages, and think how we shall take
    Our own calm journey on for human sake.

Leigh Hunt

THE RELEASE

All day he shoves the pasteboard in
The slick machine that turns out boxes,
A box a minute; and its din
Is all his music, as he stands
And feeds it; while his jaded brain
Moves only out and in again
With the slick motion of his hands,
Monotonously making boxes,
A box a minute—all his thoughts
A slick succession of empty boxes.
But, when night comes, and he is free
To play his fiddle, with the music
His whole soul moves to melody;
No more recalling day's dumb round,
His reckless spirit sweeps and whirls
On surging waves and dizzy swirls
And eddies of enchanted sound;
And in a flame-winged flight of music
Above the roofs and chimneys soars
To ride the starry tides of music.

W. W. Gibson

RAIN AT DAWN

At dawn the crickets shrill, then cease their 'plain,
The dying candle flickers through my eaves;
Though windows bar the wild dust and the rain,
I hear the drip, drip, dripping on the broad banana leaves.

Po Chu-I

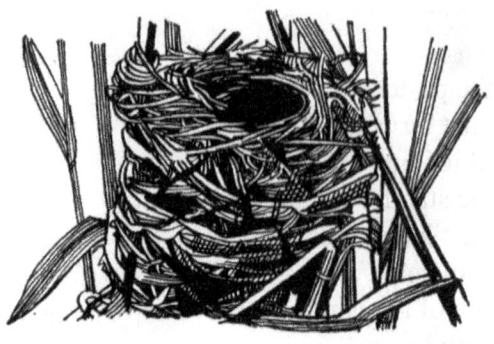

ARTISTS (*From* 'Instinctive Genius and Diligence')

But most of all it wins my admiration
To view the structure of this little work,
A bird's nest. Mark it well, within, without.
No tool had he that wrought, no knife to cut,
No nail to fix, no bodkin to insert,
No glue to join; his little beak was all,
And yet how neatly finish'd! What nice hand,
And every implement and means of art,
And twenty years' apprenticeship to boot,
Could make me such another? Fondly then
We boast of excellence, whose noblest skill
Instinctive genius foils.

The bee observe.
She too an artist is, and laughs at man,
Who calls on rules the sightly hexagon
With truth to form; a cunning architect,
Who at the roof begins her golden work,
And builds without foundation!

James Hurdis

Part Three

The Poet as Storyteller

THE LADY OF SHALOTT

Part I
On either side the river lie
Long fields of barley and of rye,
That clothe the wold and meet the sky;
And thro' the field the road runs by
    To many-tower'd Camelot;
And up and down the people go,
Gazing where the lilies blow
Round an island there below,
    The island of Shalott.

Willows whiten, aspens quiver,
Little breezes dusk and shiver
Thro' the wave that runs for ever
By the island in the river
    Flowing down to Camelot.
Four gray walls, and four gray towers
Overlook a space of flowers,
And the silent isle embowers
    The Lady of Shalott.

By the margin, willow-veil'd,
Slide the heavy barges trail'd
By slow horses; and unhail'd
The shallop flitteth, silken sail'd

Skimming down to Camelot:
But who hath seen her wave her hand?
Or at the casement seen her stand?
Or is she known in all the land,
    The Lady of Shalott?

Only reapers, reaping early
In among the bearded barley,
Hear a song that echoes cheerly
From the river winding clearly,
    Down to tower'd Camelot:
And by the moon the reaper weary,
Piling sheaves in uplands airy,
Listening, whispers, "'Tis the fairy
    Lady of Shalott."

Part II
There she weaves by night and day
A magic web with colours gay.
She has heard a whisper say,
A curse is on her if she stay
    To look down to Camelot.
She knows not what the curse may be.
And so she weaveth steadily,
And little other care hath she,
    The Lady of Shalott.

And moving thro' a mirror clear
That hangs before her all the year,
Shadows of the world appear,
There she sees the highway near
    Winding down to Camelot:
There the river eddy whirls,
And there the surly village-churls,
And the red cloaks of market girls,
    Pass onward from Shalott.

Sometimes a troop of damsels glad,
An abbot on an ambling pad,
Sometimes a curly shepherd-lad,
Or long-hair'd page in crimson clad,
    Goes by to tower'd Camelot;
And sometimes thro' the mirror blue
The knights come riding two and two:
She hath no loyal knight and true,
    The Lady of Shalott.

But in her web she still delights
To weave the mirror's magic sights,
For often thro' the silent nights
A funeral, with plumes and lights,
    And music, went to Camelot:
Or when the moon was overhead,
Came two young lovers lately wed;
"I am half sick of shadows," said
    The Lady of Shalott.

Part III
A bow-shot from her bower eaves,
He rode between the barley-sheaves,
The sun came dazzling thro' the leaves,
And flamed upon the brazen greaves
    Of bold Sir Lancelot.
A red-cross knight for ever kneel'd
To a lady in his shield,
That sparkled on the yellow field
    Beside remote Shalott.

The gemmy bridle glitter'd free,
Like to some branch of stars we see
Hung in the golden Galaxy.
The bridle bells rang merrily
    As he rode down to Camelot:

And from his blazon'd baldric slung
A mighty silver bugle hung,
And as he rode his armour rung,
   Beside remote Shalott.

All in the blue unclouded weather
Thick-jewell'd shone the saddle-leather,
The helmet and the helmet-feather
Burn'd like one burning flame together,
   As he rode down to Camelot.
As often thro' the purple night,
Below the starry clusters bright,
Some bearded meteor, trailing light,
   Moves over still Shalott.

His broad clear brow in sunlight glow'd;
On burnish'd hooves his war-horse trode,
From underneath his helmet flow'd
His coal-black curls as on he rode,
   As he rode down to Camelot.

From the bank and from the river
He flash'd into the crystal mirror,
"Tirra lirra," by the river
   Sang Sir Lancelot.

She left the web, she left the loom,
She made three paces thro' the room,
She saw the water-lily bloom,
She saw the helmet and the plume,
   She look'd down to Camelot.
Out flew the web and floated wide;
The mirror crack'd from side to side;
"The curse is come upon me," cried
   The Lady of Shalott.

Part IV
In the stormy east-wind straining,
The pale yellow woods were waning,
The broad stream in his banks complaining,
Heavily the low sky raining
   Over tower'd Camelot;
Down she came and found a boat
Beneath a willow left afloat,
And round about the prow she wrote
   "The Lady of Shalott".

And down the river's dim expanse—
Like some bold seer in a trance,
Seeing all his own mischance—
With a glassy countenance
   Did she look to Camelot.
And at the closing of the day
She loosed the chain, and down she lay;
The broad stream bore her far away,
   The Lady of Shalott.

Lying, robed in snowy white
That loosely flew to left and right—
The leaves upon her falling light—
Thro' the noises of the night
    She floated down to Camelot:
And as the boat-head wound along
The willowy hills and fields among,
They heard her singing her last song,
    The Lady of Shalott.

Heard a carol, mournful, holy,
Chanted loudly, chanted lowly,
Till her blood was frozen slowly,
And her eyes were darken'd wholly,
    Turn'd to tower'd Camelot;
For ere she reach'd upon the tide
The first house by the water-side,
Singing in her song she died,
    The Lady of Shalott.

Under tower and balcony,
By garden-wall and gallery,
A gleaming shape she floated by,
Dead-pale between the houses high,
    Silent into Camelot.
Out upon the wharfs they came,
Knight and burgher, lord and dame,
And round the prow they read her name,
    "The Lady of Shalott".

Who is this? and what is here?
And in the lighted palace near
Died the sound of royal cheer;
And they cross'd themselves for fear,
    All the knights at Camelot:

But Lancelot mused a little space;
He said, "She has a lovely face;
God in his mercy lend her grace,
   The Lady of Shalott."

Alfred, Lord Tennyson

OLD MAN TRAVELLING

   The little hedge-row birds,
That peck along the road, regard him not.
He travels on, and in his face, his step,
His gait, is one expression; every limb,
His look and bending figure, all bespeak
A man who does not move with pain, but moves
With thought—He is insensibly subdued
To settled quiet: he is one by whom
All effort seems forgotten, one to whom
Long patience has such mild composure given,
That patience now doth seem a thing, of which
He hath no need. He is by nature led
To peace so perfect, that the young behold
With envy, what the old man hardly feels.
I asked him whither he was bound, and what
The object of his journey; he replied
"Sir! I am going many miles to take
A last leave of my son, a mariner,
Who from a sea-fight has been brought to Falmouth,
And there is dying in an hospital."

William Wordsworth

THE HIGHWAYMAN

Part I
The wind was a torrent of darkness among the gusty trees,
The moon was a ghostly galleon tossed upon cloudy seas.
The road was a ribbon of moonlight over the purple moor,
And the highwayman came riding—
    Riding—riding—
The highwayman came riding, up to the old inn-door.

He'd a French cocked-hat on his forehead, a bunch of lace at his chin,
A coat of the claret velvet, and breeches of brown doe-skin.
They fitted with never a wrinkle. His boots were up to the thigh.
And he rode with a jewelled twinkle,
    His pistol butts a-twinkle,
His rapier hilt a-twinkle, under the jewelled sky.

Over the cobbles he clattered and clashed in the dark inn-yard.
He tapped with his whip on the shutters, but all was locked and barred.
He whistled a tune to the window, and who should be waiting there
But the landlord's black-eyed daughter,
    Bess, the landlord's daughter,
Plaiting a dark red love-knot into her long black hair.

And dark in the dark old inn-yard a stable-wicket creaked
Where Tim the ostler listened. His face was white and
   peaked.
His eyes were hollows of madness, his hair like mouldy
   hay,
But he loved the landlord's daughter,
The landlord's red-lipped daughter.

Dumb as a dog he listened, and he heard the robber say—
"One kiss my bonny sweetheart, I'm after a prize to-night,
But I shall be back with the yellow gold before the morning
   light;
Yet, if they press me sharply, and harry me through the
   day,
Then look for me by moonlight,
   Watch for me by moonlight,
I'll come to thee by moonlight, though hell should bar the
   way."

He rose upright in the stirrups. He scarce could reach her
   hand,
But she loosened her hair i' the casement. His face burnt
   like a brand
As the black cascade of perfume came tumbling over his
   breast;
And he kissed its waves in the moonlight,
(Oh, sweet black waves in the moonlight!)
Then he tugged at his rein in the moonlight, and galloped
   away to the west.

Part II
He did not come in the dawning. He did not come at noon;
And out o' the tawny sunset, before the rise o' the moon,
When the road was a gipsy's ribbon, looping the purple
   moor,
A red-coat troop came marching—
   Marching—marching—

King George's men came marching, up to the old inn-door.
They said no word to the landlord. They drank his ale
  instead.
But they gagged his daughter, and bound her, to the foot of
  her narrow bed.
Two of them knelt at her casement, with muskets at their
  side!
There was death at every window;
   And hell at one dark window;
For Bess could see, through her casement, the road that he
  would ride.

They had tied her up to attention, with many a sniggering
  jest.
They had bound a musket beside her, with the muzzle
  beneath her breast!
"Now, keep good watch!" and they kissed her.
She heard the dead man say—
Look for me by moonlight;
   Watch for me by moonlight;
I'll come to thee by moonlight, though hell should bar the
way!

She twisted her hands behind her; but all the knots held
  good!
She writhed her hands till her fingers were wet with sweat
  or blood!
They stretched and strained in the darkness, and the hours
  crawled by like years,
Till, now, on the stroke of midnight,
   Cold, on the stroke of midnight,
The tip of one finger touched it! The trigger at least was
  hers!

The tip of one finger touched it. She strove no more for the
   rest.
Up, she stood up to attention, with the muzzle beneath her
   breast.
She would not risk their hearing; she would not strive
   again;
For the road lay bare in the moonlight;
   Blank and bare in the moonlight;
And the blood of her veins, in the moonlight, throbbed to
   her love's refrain.

Tlot-tlot; tlot-tlot! Had they heard it? The horse-hoofs
   ringing clear;
Tlot-tlot, tlot-tlot, in the distance? Were they deaf that they
   did not hear?
Down the ribbon of moonlight, over the brow of the hill,
The highwayman came riding,
   Riding, riding!
The red-coats looked to their priming! She stood up,
   straight and still.

Tlot-tlot, in the frosty silence! Tlot-tlot, in the echoing
    night!
Nearer he came and nearer. Her face was like a light.
Her eyes grew wide for a moment; she drew one last deep
    breath,
Then her finger moved in the moonlight,
    Her musket shattered the moonlight,
Shattered her breast in the moonlight and warned him—
    with her death.

He turned. He spurred to the west; he did not know who
    stood
Bowed, with her head o'er the musket, drenched with her
    own blood!
Not till the dawn he heard it, and his face grew grey to hear
How Bess, the landlord's daughter,
    The landlord's black-eyed daughter,
Had watched for her love in the moonlight, and died in the
    darkness there.

Back he spurred like a madman, shouting a curse to the
    sky,
With the white road smoking behind him and his rapier
    brandished high.
Blood-red were his spurs i' the golden noon; wine-red was
    his velvet coat;
When they shot him down on the highway,
    Down like a dog on the highway,
And he lay in his blood on the highway, with the bunch of
    lace at his throat.

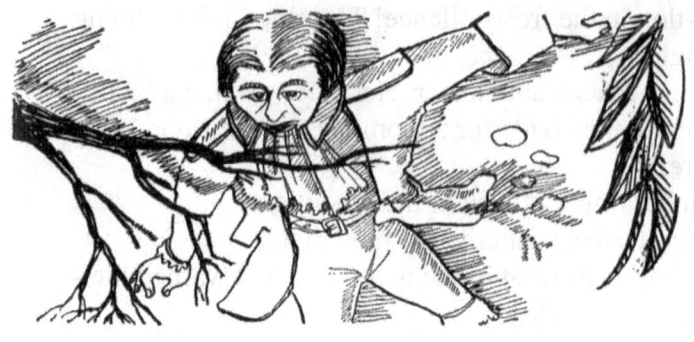

And still of a winter's night, they say, when the wind is in
    the trees,
When the moon is a ghostly galleon tossed upon cloudy
    seas,
When the road is a ribbon of moonlight over the purple
    moor,
A highwayman comes riding—
    Riding—riding—
A highwayman comes riding, up to the old inn-door.

Over the cobbles he clatters and clangs in the dark inn-
    yard.
And he taps with his whip on the shutters, but all is locked
    and barred.
He whistles a tune to the window, and who should be
    waiting there
But the landlord's black-eyed daughter,
    Bess, the landlord's daughter,
Plaiting a dark red love-knot into her long black hair.

Alfred Noyes

THE SOLDIER

Home furthest off grows dearer from the way;
And when the army in the Indies lay
Friend's letters coming from his native place
Were like old neighbours with their country face.
And every opportunity that came
Opened the sheet to gaze upon the name
Of that loved village where he left his sheep
For more contented peaceful folk to keep;
And friendly faces absent many a year
Would from such letters in his mind appear.
And when his pockets, chafing through the case,
Wore it quite out ere others took the place,
Right loath to be of company bereft
He kept the fragments while a bit was left.

John Clare

THE SHAWL

Nimble hands in Lhudiana wrought the colours of the sea,
And the floating mists of mountains in a soft shawl for me;
All the changeful light of rivers and the sunset gleam of
    spires
Flashing in a topaz heaven when the long day tires.

When the corn in Lhudiana waved in endless grey and
    green,
She began this shawl of wonder, weaving what her eyes
    had seen,
Gloom and light and gold and ebon, mirrored skies in
    gleaming pools,
Choosing silks of rainbow splendour, dazzling beads,
triumphant wools.

And her mother praised her daily, saying, "When the
    merchants come
They will marvel at its beauty, they will offer such a sum
That thy heart will fall a-trembling," and the maiden bent
    her head,
Joyful that her hands were cunning weaving miracles of
    thread.

When the fields in Lhudiana were ablaze with golden
    wheat
The last lovely silk was woven and the shawl of shawls
    complete,
Oh, the purple and the sapphire, and the light of Eastern
    seas!
And the merchant—counting gravely—gave the mother
    ten rupees.

W. Kean Seymour

MEETING AT NIGHT

The grey sea and the long black land;
And the yellow half-moon large and low;
And the startled little waves that leap
In fiery ringlets from their sleep,
As I gain the cove with pushing prow,
And quench its speed in the slushy sand.

Then a mile of warm sea-scented beach;
Three fields to cross till a farm appears;
A tap at the pane, the quick sharp scratch
A blue spurt of a lighted match,
And a voice less loud, thro' its joys and fears,
Than the two hearts beating each to each!

Robert Browning

THE DESTRUCTION OF SENNACHERIB

The Assyrian came down like the wolf on the fold,
And his cohorts were gleaming in purple and gold;
And the sheen of their spears was like stars on the sea,
When the blue wave rolls nightly on deep Galilee.

Like the leaves of the forest when Summer is green,
That host with their banners at sunset were seen:
Like the leaves of the forest when Autumn hath blown,
That host on the morrow lay wither'd and strown.

For the Angel of Death spread his wings on the blast,
And breathed in the face of the foe as he pass'd;
And the eyes of the sleepers wax'd deadly and chill,
And their hearts but once heaved, and for ever grew still!

And there lay the steed with his nostril all wide,
But through it there roll'd not the breath of his pride;
And the foam of his gasping lay white on the turf,
And cold as the spray of the rock-beating surf.

And there lay the rider distorted and pale,
With the dew on his brow, and the rust on his mail:
And the tents were all silent, the banners alone,
The lances unlifted, the trumpet unblown.

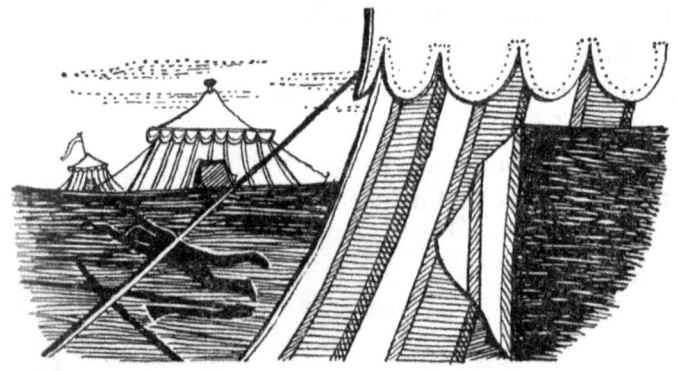

And the widows of Ashur are loud in their wail,
And the idols are broke in the temple of Baal;
And the might of the Gentile, unsmote by the sword,
Hath melted like snow in the glance of the Lord!

Lord Byron

PARTING AT MORNING

Round the cape of a sudden came the sea,
And the sun looked over the mountain's rim:
And straight was a path of gold for him,
And the need of a world of men for me.

Robert Browning

JAFFÀR

Jaffàr, the Barmecide, the good Vizier,
The poor man's hope, the friend without a peer,
Jaffàr was dead, slain by a doom unjust;
And guilty Haroun, sullen with mistrust
Of what the good and e'en the bad might say,
Ordained that no man living from that day
Should dare to speak his name on pain of death—
All Araby and Persia held their breath,

All but the brave Mondeer—He, proud to show
How far for love a grateful soul could go,
And facing death for very scorn and grief,
(For his great heart wanted a great relief),
Stood forth in Bagdad, daily in the square
Where once had stood a happy house, and there
Harangued the tremblers at the scymitar
On all they owed to the divine Jaffàr.

"Bring me this man," the caliph cried. The man
Was brought—was gazed upon. The mutes began
To bind his arms. "Welcome, brave cords," cried he;
"From bonds far worse Jaffàr delivered me;
From wants, from shames, from loveless household fears;
Made a man's eyes friends with delicious tears;
Restored me, loved me, put me on a par
With his great self. How can I pay Jaffàr?"

Haroun, who felt that on a soul like this
The mightiest vengeance could but fall amiss,
Now deigned to smile, as one great lord of fate
Might smile upon another half as great.
He said, "Let worth grow frenzied, if it will;
The caliph's judgement shall be master still.
Go: and since gifts so move thee, take this gem,
The richest in the Tartar's diadem,

And hold the giver as thou deemest fit."

"Gifts!" cried the friend. He took; and holding it
High towards the heavens, as though to meet his star,
Exclaimed, "This too I owe to thee, Jaffàr."

Leigh Hunt

STILL WATERS

Says Tweed to Till,
"What makes you run so still?"
Says Till to Tweed,
"Though you run with speed,
    And I run slow,
For every man that you drown,
    I drown two!"

Anon.

GOLIATH

Still as a mountain with dark pines and sun
He stood between the armies, and his shout
Rolled from the empyrean above the host:
"Bid any little flea ye have come forth,
And wince at death upon my finger-nail!"
He turned his large-boned face; and all his steel
Tossed into beams the lustre of the noon;
And all the shaggy horror of his locks
Rustled like locusts in a field of corn.
The meagre pupil of his shameless eye
Moved like a cormorant over a glassy sea.

He stretched his limbs, and laughed into the air,
To feel the groaning sinews of his breast,
And the long gush of his swollen arteries pause:
And, nodding, wheeled, towering in all his height.
Then like a wind that hushes, he gazed and saw
Down, down, far down upon the untroubled green
A shepherd-boy that swung a little sling.
Goliath shut his lids to drive that mote
Which vexed the eastern azure of his eye
Out of his vision; and stared down again.
Yet stood the youth there, ruddy in the flare
Of his vast shield, nor spake, nor quailed, gazed up
As one might scan a mountain to be scaled.
Then, as it were, a voice unearthly still
Cried in the cavern of his bristling ear,
"His name is Death!" . . . And, like the flush
That dyes Sahara to its lifeless verge,
His brows bright brass flamed into sudden crimson;
And his great spear leapt upward, lightning-like,
Shaking a dreadful thunder in the air;
Span betwixt earth and sky, bright as a berg
That hoards the sunlight in a myriad spires,
Crashed: and struck echo through an army's heart.
Then paused Goliath, and stared down again.
And fleet-foot Fear from rolling orbs perceived
Steadfast, unharmed, a stooping shepherd-boy
Frowning upon the target of his face.
And wrath tossed suddenly up once more his hand;
And a deep groan grieved all his strength in him.
He breathed; and, lost in dazzling darkness, prayed—
Besought his reins, his gloating gods, his youth:
And turned to smite what he no more could see.

Then sped the singing pebble-messenger,
The chosen of the Lord from Israel's brooks,
Fleet to its mark, and hollowed a light path
Down to the appalling Babel of his brain.
And like the smoke of dreaming Souffriere
Dust rose in cloud, spread wide, slow silted down
Softly all softly on his armour's blaze.

Walter De La Mare

From SOHRAB AND RUSTUM

He spoke; and Sohrab kindled at his taunts,
And he too drew his sword: at once they rush'd
Together, as two eagles on one prey
Come rushing down together from the clouds,
One from the east, one from the west: their shields
Dash'd with a clang together, and a din
Rose, such as that the sinewy woodcutters
Make often in the forest's heart at morn,
Of hewing axes, crashing trees: such blows
Rustum and Sohrab on each other hail'd.
And you would say that sun and stars took part
In that unnatural conflict; for a cloud
Grew suddenly in Heaven, and dark'd the sun
Over the fighters' heads; and a wind rose

Under their feet, and moaning swept the plain,
And in a sandy whirlwind wrapp'd the pair.
In gloom they twain were wrapp'd, and they alone;
For both the on-looking hosts on either hand
Stood in broad daylight, and the sky was pure,
And the sun sparkled on the Oxus stream.
But in the gloom they fought, with bloodshot eyes
And labouring breath; first Rustum struck the shield
Which Sohrab held stiff out: the steel-spiked spear
Rent the tough plates, but fail'd to reach the skin,
And Rustum pluck'd it back with angry groan.
Then Sohrab with his sword smote Rustum's helm,
Nor clove its steel quite through; but all the crest
He shore away, and that proud horsehair plume,
Never till now defil'd sunk to the dust;
And Rustum bow'd his head; but then the gloom
Grew blacker: thunder rumbled in the air,
And lightnings rent the cloud; and Ruksh, the horse,
Who stood at hand, utter'd a dreadful cry:
No horse's cry was that, most like the roar
Of some pain'd desert lion, who all day
Has trail'd the hunter's javelin in his side,
And comes at night to die upon the sand:
The two hosts heard that cry, and quak'd for fear,
And Oxus curdled as it cross'd his stream.
But Sohrab heard, and quail'd not, but rush'd on,
And struck again; and again Rustum bow'd
His head; but this time all the blade, like glass,
Sprang in a thousand shivers on the helm,
And in his hand the hilt remain'd alone.
Then Rustum rais'd his head: his dreadful eyes
Glar'd, and he shook on high his menacing spear,
And shouted, *Rustum!* Sohrab heard that shout.
And shrank amaz'd: back he recoil'd one step,
And scanned with blinking eyes the advancing Form:
And then he stood bewilder'd; and he dropp'd
His covering shield, and the spear pierc'd his side,

He reel'd, and staggering back, sunk to the ground, and the
   wind fell,
And the bright sun broke forth, and melted all
The cloud; and the two armies saw the pair;
Saw Rustum standing, safe upon his feet,
And Sohrab, wounded, on the bloody sand.

Matthew Arnold

HOW THEY BROUGHT THE GOOD NEWS FROM GHENT TO AIX

I sprang to the stirrup, and Joris, and he;
I galloped, Dirck galloped, we galloped all three;
"Good speed!" cried the watch, as the gate-bolts undrew;
"Speed!" echoed the wall to us galloping through;
Behind shut the postern, the lights sank to rest,
And into the midnight we galloped abreast.

Not a word to each other; we kept the great pace
Neck by neck, stride by stride, never changing our place;
I turned in my saddle and made its girths tight,
Then shortened each stirrup, and set the pique right,
Rebuckled the cheek-strap, chained slacker the bit,
Nor galloped less steadily Roland a whit.

'Twas moonset at starting; but while we drew near
Lokeren, the cocks crew and twilight dawned clear;
At Boom, a great yellow star came out to see;
At Duffeld, 'twas morning as plain as could be;
And from Mecheln church-steeple we heard the half-chime,
So Joris broke silence with, "Yet there is time!"

At Aershot, up leaped of a sudden the sun,
And against him the cattle stood black every one,
To stare thro' the mist at us galloping past,
And I saw my stout galloper Roland at last
With resolute shoulders, each butting away
The haze, as some bluff river headlong its spray.

And his low head and crest, just one sharp ear bent back
For my voice, and the other pricked out on his track;
And one eye's black intelligence—ever that glance
O'er its white edge at me, his own master, askance!
And the thick heavy spume-flakes which aye and anon
His fierce lips shook upwards in galloping on.

By Hasselt, Dirck groaned; and cried Joris, "Stay spur!
Your Roos galloped bravely, the fault's not in her.
We'll remember at Aix"—for one heard the quick wheeze
Of her chest, saw the stretched neck and staggering knees,
And sunk tail, and horrible heave of the flank,
As down on her haunches she shuddered and sank.

So we were left galloping, Joris and I,
Past Looz and past Tongres, no cloud in the sky!
The broad sun above laughed a pitiless laugh,
'Neath our feet broke the brittle, bright stubble like chaff;
Till over by Dalhem a dome-spire sprang white,
And "Gallop," gasped Joris, "for Aix is in sight!"

"How they'll greet us!" and all in a moment his roan
Rolled neck and croup over, lay dead as a stone;
And there was my Roland to bear the whole weight
Of the news which alone could save Aix from her fate,
With his nostrils like pits full of blood to the brim,
And with circles of red for his eye-sockets' rim.

Then I cast loose my buffcoat, each holster let fall,
Shook off both my jack-boots, let go belt and all,
Stood up in the stirrup, leaned, patted his ear,
Called my Roland his pet-name, my horse without peer;
Clapped my hands, laughed and sang, any noise, bad or good,
Till at length into Aix Roland galloped and stood.

And all I remember is—friends flocking round,
As I sate with his head 'twixt my knees on the ground,
And no voice but was praising this Roland of mine,
As I poured down his throat our last measure of wine
Which (the burgesses voted by common consent)
Was no more than his due who brought good news from Ghent.

Robert Browning

KUBLA KHAN

In Xanadu did Kubla Khan
A stately pleasure-dome decree:
Where Alph, the sacred river, ran
Through caverns measureless to man
    Down to a sunless sea.
So twice five miles of fertile ground
With walls and towers were girdled round:
And there were gardens bright with sinuous rills,
Where blossomed many an incense-bearing tree;
And here were forests ancient as the hills,
Enfolding sunny spots of greenery.

But oh! that deep romantic chasm which slanted
Down the green hill athwart a cedarn cover!
A savage place! as holy and enchanted
As e'er beneath a waning moon was haunted
By woman wailing for her demon-lover!
And from this chasm, with ceaseless turmoil seething,
As if this earth in fast thick pants were breathing,
A mighty fountain momently was forced:
Amid whose swift half-intermitted burst
Huge fragments vaulted like rebounding hail,
Or chaffy grain beneath the thresher's flail:
And 'mid these dancing rocks at once and ever
It flung up momently the sacred river.
Five miles meandering with a mazy motion
Through wood and dale the sacred river ran,
Then reached the caverns measureless to man,
And sank in tumult to a lifeless ocean:
And 'mid this tumult Kubla heard from far
Ancestral voices prophesying war!
    The shadow of the dome of pleasure
    Floated midway on the waves;
    Where was heard the mingled measure
    From the fountain and the caves.

It was a miracle of rare device,
A sunny pleasure-dome with caves of ice!

   A damsel with a dulcimer
   In a vision once I saw:
   It was an Abyssinian maid,
   And on her dulcimer she played,
   Singing of Mount Abora.
   Could I revive within me
   Her symphony and song,
   To such a deep delight 'twould win me,
   That with music loud and long,
   I would build that dome in air,
   That sunny dome! those caves of ice!
And all who heard should see them there,
And all should cry, "Beware! Beware!
   His flashing eyes, his floating hair!
   Weave a circle round him thrice,
   And close your eyes with holy dread,
   For he on honey-dew hath fed,
   And drunk the milk of Paradise."

S. T. Coleridge

AFTER BLENHEIM

It was a summer evening,
   Old Kaspar's work was done,
And he before his cottage door
   Was sitting in the sun:
And by him sported on the green
His little grandchild Wilhelmine.

She saw her brother Peterkin
    Roll something large and round
Which he beside the rivulet
    In playing there had found:
He came to ask what he had found
That was so large and smooth and round.

Old Kaspar took it from the boy
    Who stood expectant by;
And then the old man shook his head,
    And with a natural sigh,
"'Tis some poor fellow's skull," said he,
"Who fell in the great victory.

"I find them in the garden,
    For there's many here about;
And often when I go to plough
    The ploughshare turns them out.
For many thousand men," said he,
"Were slain in that great victory."

"Now tell us what 'twas all about."
    Young Peterkin he cries;
And little Wilhelmine looks up
    With wonder-waiting eyes;
"Now tell us all about the war,
And what they fought each other for."

"It was the English," Kaspar cried,
    "Who put the French to rout;
But what they fought each other for
    I could not well make out.
But everybody said," quoth he,
"That 'twas a famous victory.

"My father lived at Blenheim then,
    Yon little stream hard by;
They burnt his dwelling to the ground,
    And he was forced to fly;
So with his wife and child he fled,
Nor had he where to rest his head.

"With fire and sword the country round
    Was wasted far and wide,
And many a childing mother then
    And newborn baby died:
But things like that, you know, must be
At every famous victory.

"They say it was a shocking sight
    After the field was won;
For many thousand bodies here
    Lay rotting in the sun;
But things like that, you know, must be
After a famous victory.

"Great praise the Duke of Marlboro' won
    And our good Prince Eugene,"
"Why, 'twas a very wicked thing!"
    Said little Wilhelmine;

"Nay . . . nay . . . my little girl," quoth he,
"It was a famous victory.

"And everybody praised the Duke
   Who this great fight did win."
"But what good came of it at last?"
   Quoth little Peterkin:
"Why that I cannot tell," said he,
"But 'twas a famous victory."
*Robert
Southey*

THE ROSE

A rose, as fair as ever saw the North,
Grew in a little garden all alone;
A sweeter flower did Nature ne'er put forth,
Nor fairer garden yet was never known:

The maidens danced about it morn and noon,
And learned bards of it their ditties made;
The nimble fairies by the pale-faced moon
Watered the root and kissed her pretty shade.

But well-a-day! the gardener careless grew;
The maids and fairies were both kept away,
And in a drought the caterpillars threw
Themselves upon the bud and every spray.

God shield the stock! If heaven send no supplies,
The fairest blossom of the garden dies.

William Browne

From MY LOST YOUTH

Often I think of the beautiful town
    That is seated beside the sea;
Often in thought go up and down
The pleasant streets of that dear old town,
    And my youth comes back to me.
        And a verse of a Lapland song
           Is haunting my memory still:
"A boy's will is the wind's will,
And the thoughts of youth are long, long thoughts."

I can see the shadowy lines of its trees,
    And catch in sudden gleams,
The sheen of the far-surrounding seas,
The islands that were the Hesperides
    Of all my boyish dreams.
        And the burden of that old song,
           It murmurs and whispers still:
"A boy's will is the wind's will,
And the thoughts of youth are long, long thoughts."

I remember the black wharves and the slips,
    And the sea-tides tossing free;
And the Spanish sailors with bearded lips,
And the beauty and mystery of the ships,
    And the magic of the sea.
And the voice of that wayward song
        Is singing and saying still:
"A boy's will is the wind's will,
And the thoughts of youth are long, long thoughts."

I remember the bulwarks by the shore,
    And the fort upon the hill;
The sunrise gun, with its hollow roar,
The drum-beat repeated o'er and o'er,
    And the bugle wild and shrill.
        And the music of that old song
        Throbs in my memory still:
"A boy's will is the wind's will,
And the thoughts of youth are long, long thoughts."

I remember the sea-fight far away,
    How it thundered o'er the tide!
And the dead captains, as they lay
In their graves, o'erlooking the tranquil bay,
    Where they in battle died.
        And the sound of that mournful song
        Goes through me with a thrill:
"A boy's will is the wind's will,
And the thoughts of youth are long, long thoughts."

I remember the gleams and glooms that dart
    Across the schoolboy's brain;
The song and the silence in the heart,
That in part are prophecies, and in part
    Are longings wild and vain.
        And the voice of that fitful song
        Sings on, and is never still:
"A boy's will is the wind's will,
And the thoughts of youth are long, long thoughts."

H. W. Longfellow

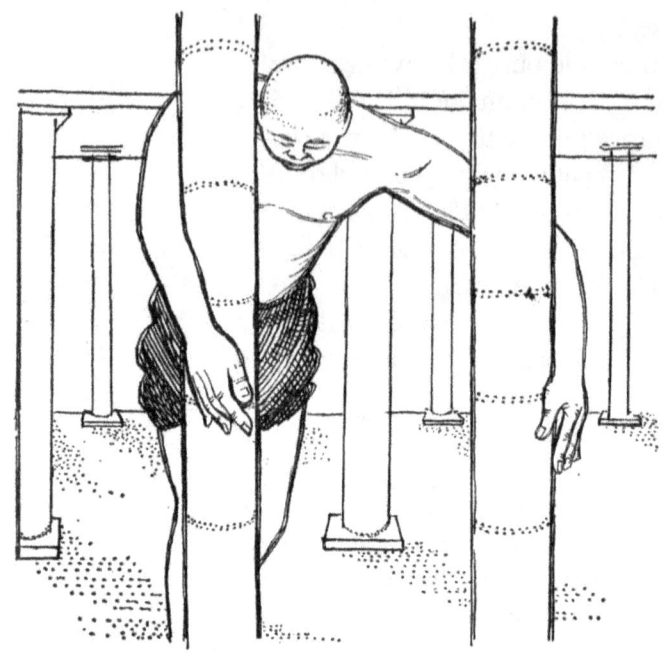

THE DEATH OF SAMSON *From* 'Samson Agonistes'

A Messenger Speaks:
Occasions drew me early to this city,
And as the gates I entered with sunrise,
The morning trumpets festival proclaimed
Through each high street. Little I had dispatched,
When all abroad was rumoured, that this day
Samson should be brought forth to show the people
Proof of his mighty strength in feats and games;
I sorrowed at his captive state, but minded
Not to be absent at that spectacle.
The building was a spacious theatre,
Half-round, on two main pillars vaulted high,
With seats, where all the lords and each degree
Of sort might sit in order to behold;
The other side was open where the throng
On banks and scaffolds under sky might stand;

I among these aloof obscurely stood.
The feast and noon grew high, and sacrifice
Had filled their hearts with mirth, high cheer and wine,
When to their sports they turned. Immediately
Was Samson as a public servant brought,
In their state livery clad; before him pipes
And timbrels, on each side went armed guards,
Both horse and foot, before him and behind
Archers, and slingers, cataphracts, and spears.
At sight of him the people with a shout
Rifted the air, clamouring their god with praise,
Who had made their dreadful enemy their thrall.
He patient, but undaunted, where they led him,
Came to the place, and what was set before him,
Which without help of eye might be assayed,
To heave, pull, draw, or break, he still performed,
All with incredible stupendous force,
None daring to appear antagonist.
At length, for intermission sake, they led him
Between the pillars; he his guide requested,
For so from such as nearer stood we heard,
As over-tired, to let him lean awhile
With both his arms on those two massy pillars,
That to the arched roof gave main support,
He, unsuspicious, led him; which when Samson
Felt in his arms, with head awhile inclined,
And eyes fast fixed he stood, as one who prayed,
Or some great matter in his mind revolved:
At last, with head erect, thus cried aloud:
"Hitherto, lords, what your commands imposed
I have performed, as reason was, obeying,
Not without wonder or delight beheld:
Now of my own accord such other trial
I mean to show you of my strength, yet greater;
As with amaze shall strike all who behold."
This uttered, straining all his nerves, he bowed.
As with the force of winds and waters pent,

When mountains tremble, those two massy pillars
With horrible convulsion to and fro
He tugged, he shook, till down they came, and drew
The whole roof after them, with burst of thunder,
Upon the heads of all who sat beneath,
Lords, ladies, captains, counsellors, or priests
Their choice nobility and flower, not only
Of this, but each Philistian city round,
Met from all parts to solemnize this feast.
Samson, with these inmixed, inevitably
Pulled down the same destruction on himself.

John Milton

THE EASTERN GATE

A poor man determines to go out into the world and make his fortune. His wife tries to detain him.

I went out at the eastern gate:
I never thought to return.
But I came back to the gate with my heart full of sorrow.
There was not a peck of rice in the bin:
There was not a coat hanging on the pegs.
So I took my sword and went towards the gate.

My wife and child clutched at my coat and wept:
"Some people want to be rich and grand:
I only want to share my porridge with you.
Above, we have the blue waves of the sky:
Below, the yellow face of this little child."
    "Dear wife, I cannot stay.
    Soon it will be too late.
    When one is growing old
    One cannot put things off."

Anon.

LA BELLE DAME SANS MERCI

"O what can ail thee, knight-at-arms,
    Alone and palely loitering?
The sedge has withered from the lake,
    And no birds sing.

"O what can ail thee knight-at-arms!
    So haggard and so woe-begone?
The squirrel's granary is full,
    And the harvest's done.

"I see a lily on thy brow
    With anguish moist and fever-dew,
And on thy cheeks a fading rose
    Fast withereth too."

"I met a lady in the meads,
    Full beautiful—a fairy's child,
Her hair was long, her foot was light,
    And her eyes were wild.

"I made a garland for her head,
    And bracelets too, and fragrant zone;
She look'd at me as she did love,
    And made sweet moan.

"I set her on my pacing steed
    And nothing else saw all day long,
For sidelong would she bend, and sing
    A fairy's song.

"She found me roots of relish sweet
    And honey wild and manna-dew,
And sure in language strange she said,
    'I love thee true.'

"She took me to her elfin grot,
    And there she wept and sigh'd full sore,
And there I shut her wild, wild eyes
    With kisses four.

"And there she lulled me asleep,
    And there I dream'd—Ah! woe betide!
The latest dream I ever dream'd
    On the cold hill's side.

"I saw pale kings and princes too,
    Pale warriors, death-pale were they all,
They cried—'La Belle Dame Sans
    Merci Hath thee in thrall!'

"I saw their starved lips in the gloam
    With horrid warning gaped wide,
And I awoke and found me here
    On the cold hill's side.

"And this is why I sojourn here
    Alone and palely loitering,
Though the sedge is wither'd from the lake,
    And no birds sing."

John Keats

THE CAP AND BELLS

The jester walked in the garden:
The garden had fallen still;
He bade his soul rise upward
And stand on her window-sill.

It rose in a straight blue garment,
When owls began to call:
It had grown wise-tongued by thinking
Of a quiet and light footfall;

But the young queen would not listen;
She rose in her pale night gown;
She drew in the heavy casement
And pushed the latches down.

He bade his heart go to her,
When the owls called out no more;
In a red and quivering garment
It sang to her through the door.

It had grown sweet-tongued by dreaming
Of a flutter of flower-like hair;
But she took up her fan from the table
And waved it off on the air.

"I have cap and bells," he pondered,
"I will send them to her and die";
And when the morning whitened
He left them where she went by.

She laid them upon her bosom,
Under a cloud of her hair,
And her red lips sang them a love-song
Till stars grew out of the air.

She opened her door and her window,
And the heart and the soul came through,
To her right hand came the red one,
To her left hand came the blue.
They set up a noise like crickets,
A chattering wise and sweet,
And her hair was a folded flower
And the quiet of love in her feet.

W. B. Yeats

THE GALLEY OF COUNT ARNALDOS

Ah! what pleasant visions haunt me
    As I gaze upon the sea!
All the old romantic legends,
    All my dreams, come back to me.

Sails of silk and ropes of sandal,
    Such as gleam in ancient lore;
And the singing of the sailors,
    And the answer from the shore!

Most of all, the Spanish ballad
    Haunts me oft, and tarries long,
Of the noble Count Arnaldos
    And the sailor's mystic song.

Telling how the Count Arnaldos,
    With his hawk upon his hand,
Saw a fair and stately galley,
    Steering onward to the land;

How he heard the ancient helmsman
    Chant a song so wild and clear,
That the sailing sea-bird slowly
    Poised upon the mast to hear.

Till his soul was full of longing,
    And he cried, with impulse strong,—
"Helmsman! for the love of heaven,
    Teach me, too, that wondrous song!"

"Wouldst thou,"—so the helmsman answered,
    "Learn the secret of the sea?
Only those who brave its dangers
    Comprehend its mystery!"

H. W. Longfellow

A LAKE AND A FAIRY BOAT

A lake and a fairy boat
To sail in the moonlight clear,—
And merrily we would float
From the dragons that watch us here!

Thy gown should be snow-white silk;
And strings of orient pearls,
Like gossamers dipped in milk,
Should twine with thy raven curls!

Red rubies should deck thy hands,
And diamonds should be thy dower—
But Fairies have broke their wands,
And wishing has lost its power!

Thomas Hood

THE MERMAID

I
Who would be
A mermaid fair,
Singing alone,
Combing her hair
Under the sea,
In a golden curl
With a comb of pearl
On a throne?

II
I would be a mermaid fair;
I would sing to myself the whole of the day;
With a comb of pearl I would comb my hair
And still as I comb'd I would sing and say,
"Who is it loves me? Who loves not me?"
I would comb my hair till my ringlets would fall,
    Low adown, low adown,
From under my starry sea-bud crown
    Low adown and around,
And I should look like a fountain of gold
    Springing alone
With a shrill inner sound,
    Over the throne
In the midst of the hall;

Till that great sea-snake under the sea
From his coiled sleeps in the central deeps
Would slowly trail himself sevenfold
Round the hall where I sate, and look in at the gate
With his large calm eyes for the love of me.

And all the mermen under the sea
Would feel their immortality
Die in their hearts for the love of me.

III
But at night I would wander away, away,
    I would fling on each side my low-flowing locks,
And lightly vault from the throne and play
    With the mermen in and out of the rocks;
We would run to and fro, and hide and seek,
    On the broad sea-wolds in the crimson shells,
    Whose silvery spikes are nighest the sea.
But if any came near I would call, and shriek,
And adown the steep like a wave I would leap
From the diamond ledges that jut from the dells;
For I would not be kiss'd by all who would list,
Of the bold merry mermen under the sea;
They would sue me, and woo me, and flatter me,
In the purple twilights under the sea;
But the king of them all would carry me,
Woo me, and win me, and marry me,
In the branching jaspers under the sea;
Then all the dry pied things that be
In the hueless mosses under the sea
Would curl round my silver feet silently,
All looking up for the love of me.
And if I should carol aloud, from aloft
All things that are forked, and horned, and soft
Would lean out from the hollow sphere of the sea,
All looking down for the love of me.

Alfred, Lord Tennyson

THE ENCHANTED ISLAND

To Rathlin's Isle I chanced to sail
    When summer breezes softly blew,
And there I heard so sweet a tale
    That oft I wished it could be true.

They said, at eve, when rude winds sleep,
    And hushed is ev'ry turbid swell,
A mermaid rises from the deep
    And sweetly tunes her magic shell.

And while she plays, rock, dell, and cave,
    In dying falls the sound retain,
As if some choral spirits gave
    Their aid to swell her witching strain.

Then summoned by that dulcet note,
    Uprising to th' admiring view,
A fairy island seems to float
    With tints of many a gorgeous hue.

And glittering fanes, and lofty towers,
    All on this fairy isle are seen:
And waving trees, and shady bowers,
    With more than mortal verdure green.

And as it moves, the western sky
    Glows with a thousand varying rays;
And the calm sea, tinged with each dye,
    Seems like a golden flood of haze.

They also say, if earth or stone
    From verdant Erin's hallowed land
Were on this magic island thrown,
    For ever fixed it then would stand.

But when for this some little boat
    In silence ventures from the shore,
The mermaid sinks—hushed is the note—
    The fairy isle is seen no more.

L. A. Conolly

THE ENCHANTED SHIRT

The King was sick. His cheek was red
    And his eye was clear and bright;
He ate and drank with kingly zest,
    And peacefully snored at night.

But he said he was sick, and a King should know,
    And the doctors came by the score.
They did not cure him. He cut off their heads
    And sent to the schools for more.

At last two famous doctors came,
    And one was as poor as a rat,
He had passed his life in studious toil,
    And never found time to grow fat.

The other had never looked in a book;
    His patients gave him no trouble,
If they recovered they paid him well,
    If they died their heirs paid double.

Together they looked at the royal tongue,
  As the King on his couch reclined;
In succession they thumped his august chest,
  But no trace of disease could find.

The old sage said, "You're as sound as a nut."
  "Hang him up!" roared the King in a gale,
In a ten-knot gale of royal rage;
  The other leech grew a shade pale;

But he pensively rubbed his sagacious nose,
  And thus his prescription ran—
The King will be well if he sleeps one night
  In the shirt of a Happy Man.

Wide o'er the realm the couriers rode,
  And fast their horses ran,
  And many they saw, and to many they spoke,
But they found no Happy Man.

They found poor men who would fain be rich.
    And rich who thought they were poor;
And men who twisted their waists in stays,
    And women that short-hose wore.

They saw two men by the roadside sit,
    And both bemoaned their lot;
For one had buried his wife, he said,
    And the other one had not.

At last they came to a village gate,
    A beggar lay whistling there;
He whistled and sang and laughed and rolled
    On the grass in the soft June air.

The weary couriers paused and looked
    At the scamp so blithe and gay;
And one of them said, "Heaven save you, friend,
    You seem to be happy to-day."

"O yes, fair Sirs," the rascal laughed,
    And his voice rang free and glad,
"An idle man has so much to do
    That he never has time to be sad."

"This is our man," the courier said;
    "Our luck has led us aright.
I will give you a hundred ducats, friend,
    For the loan of your shirt to-night."

The merry blackguard lay back on the grass,
    And laughed till his face was black;
"I would do it, God wot," and he roared with the fun,
    "But I haven't a shirt to my back."

Each day to the King the reports came in
    Of his unsuccessful spies,
And the sad panorama of human woes
    Passed daily under his eyes.

And he grew ashamed of his useless life,
    And his maladies hatched in gloom;
He opened his windows and let the air
    Of the free heaven into his room.

And out he went in the world and toiled
    In his own appointed way;
And the people blessed him, the land was glad,
    And the King was well and gay.

John Hay

BISHOP HATTO

The summer and autumn had been so wet
That in winter the corn was growing yet:
'Twas a piteous sight to see all around
The corn lie rotting on the ground.

Every day the starving poor
They crowded round Bishop Hatto's door,
For he had a plentiful last-year's store,
And all the neighbourhood could tell
His granaries were furnished well.

At last Bishop Hatto appointed a day
To quiet the poor without delay;
He bade them to his great barn repair,
And they should have food for the winter there.

Rejoiced such tidings good to hear,
The poor folk flock'd from far and near;
The great barn was full as it could hold
Of women and children, and young and old.

Then when he saw it could hold no more,
Bishop Hatto he made fast the door;
And whilst for mercy on Christ they call,
He set fire to the barn and burnt them all.

"I'faith 'tis an excellent bonfire!" quoth he,
"And the country is greatly obliged to me,
For ridding it in these times forlorn,
Of rats that only consume the corn."

So then to his palace returned he
And he sat down to supper merrily,
And he slept that night like an innocent man,
But Bishop Hatto never slept again.

In the morning as he enter'd the hall,
Where his picture hung against the wall,
A sweat like death all over him came,
For the rats had eaten it out of the frame.

As he look'd there came a man from his farm,
He had a countenance white with alarm;
"My lord, I open'd your granaries this morn,
And the rats had eaten all your corn."

Another came running presently,
And he was pale as pale could be,
"Fly! my Lord Bishop, fly!" quoth he,
"Ten thousand rats are coming this way—
The Lord forgive you for yesterday!"

"I'll go to my tower in the Rhine," replied he,
'Tis the safest place in Germany;
The walls are high, and the shores are steep,
And the tide is strong, and the water deep."

Bishop Hatto fearfully hasten'd away,
And he crossed the Rhine without delay,
And reach'd his tower in the island and barr'd
All the gates secure and hard.

He laid him down and closed his eyes—
But soon a scream made him arise;
He started, and saw two eyes of flame
On his pillow from whence the screaming came.

He listen'd and look'd;—it was only the cat;
But the Bishop he grew more fearful for that,
For she sat screaming mad with fear,
At the army of rats that were drawing near.

For they have swum over the river so deep,
And they have climb'd the shores so steep,
And now by thousands up they crawl;
To the holes and the window in the wall.

Down on his knees the Bishop fell,
And faster and faster his beads did he tell,
As louder and louder drawing near
The saw of their teeth without he could hear.

And in at the windows, and in at the door,
And through the walls by thousands they pour,
And down from the ceiling, and up through the floor,
From the right and the left, from behind and before,
From within and without, from above and below,
And all at once to the Bishop they go.

They have whetted their teeth against the stones,
And now they pick the Bishop's bones;
They gnaw'd the flesh from every limb,
For they were sent to do judgement on him!

Robert Southey

ON A CERTAIN LADY AT COURT

I know a thing that's most uncommon;
    (Envy, be silent and attend!)
I know a reasonable woman,
    Handsome and witty, yet a friend.

Not warp'd by passion, awed by rumour;
    Not grave through pride, nor gay through folly;
An equal mixture of good-humour
    And sensible soft melancholy.

"Has she no faults then (Envy says), Sir?"
    Yes, she has one, I must aver:
When all the world conspires to praise her,
    The woman's deaf, and does not hear.

Alexander Pope

GET UP AND BAR THE DOOR

It fell about the Martinmas time,
    And a gay time it was then,
When our goodwife got puddings to make,
    And she's boiled them in the pan.

The wind so cold blew south and north,
    And blew into the floor;
Quoth our goodman to our goodwife,
    "Get up and bar the door."

"My hand is in my household work,
    Goodman as ye may see;
And it will not be barred for a hundred years,
    If it's to be barred by me!"

They made a pact between them both,
    They made it firm and sure,
That whosoe'er should speak the first,
    Should rise and bar the door.

Then by there came two gentleman,
    At twelve o'clock at night,
And they could see neither house nor hall,
    Nor coal nor candlelight.

"Now whether is this a rich man's house,
    Or whether is it a poor?"
But never a word would one of them speak,
    For barring of the door.

The guests they ate the white puddings,
    And then they ate the black;
Tho' much the goodwife thought to herself,
    Yet never a word she spake.

Then said one stranger to the other,
    "Here, man, take ye my knife;
Do ye take off the old man's beard,
    And I'll kiss the goodwife."

"There's no hot water to scrape it off,
    And what shall we do then?"
"Then why not use the pudding broth,
    That boils into the pan?"

O up then started our goodman,
    An angry man was he:
"Will ye kiss my wife before my eyes!
    And with pudding broth scald me!"

Then up and started our goodwife,
    Gave three skips on the floor:
"Goodman, you've spoken the foremost word.
    Get up and bar the door!"

Anon.

THE PARROT: A TRUE STORY

A Parrot, from the Spanish Main,
    Full young and early caged, came o'er,
With bright wings, to the bleak domain
    Of Mulla's shore.

To spicy groves where he had won
    His plumage of resplendent hue,
His native fruits and skies and sun,
    He bade adieu.

For these he changed the smoke of turf,
    A heathery land and misty sky,
And turned on rocks and raging surf
    His golden eye.

But petted in our climate cold,
    He lived and chattered many a day:
Until with age from green and gold
    His wings grew grey.

At last, when blind, and seeming dumb,
    He scolded, laughed and spoke no more,
A Spanish stranger chanced to come
    To Mulla's shore.

He hailed the bird in Spanish speech,
    The bird in Spanish speech replied,
Flapped round his cage with joyous screech,
    Dropped down, and died.

            Thomas Campbell

INTRODUCTION TO THE TEACHING AND LEARNING NOTES AND GUIDE
BOOK FIVE

Part One of Book Five of *Poems to Enjoy* contains poems which are particularly enjoyable to read aloud. Part Two consists of a selection of descriptive poetry and Part Three provides a number of narrative poems.

A variety of material is thus provided for a variety of teaching methods. Sometimes the students can simply listen as the teacher reads aloud a number of poems, perhaps with a related, or similar theme. At other times the students may take part in the reading themselves, either individually, or in groups. When a poem is suitable, it can be discussed after the teacher has read it aloud. If it is vividly descriptive, the students can often be encouraged to sketch or paint from their imagination.

Whatever the approach, poetry can mean a great deal to Secondary School students at this stage. They should now be better equipped to understand more completely the purpose, thoughts and moods of the poet. Taste is beginning to develop and the student is starting to discriminate. The teacher can assist this development, if he introduces an interesting diversity of poetic material and if he avoids the assumption that the students ought to like certain poems, even if they do not.

The following observations are amplified in the Teaching Notes, as applied to individual poems:

1. Poems to Speak

The poems most suitable for reading aloud, whether individually, in chorus, or in groups, are those which have a pronounced rhythmic and musical quality. The choice of material is particularly important and it should be borne in mind that only certain poems are suitable for choral reading. The teacher should avoid (a) poems which are too personal in quality—e.g. many lyrics, (b) long narrative poems and (c) extensive descriptive passages, unrelieved by dialogue of any kind. Whether a poem should be spoken by the class as a whole in unison, or whether it should be said by individuals, or by groups of 'dark' or 'light' voices, depends upon the teacher and, even better, upon the agreement of students and teacher after discussion. Every poem which is at all suitable for choral work is open to much variation and the suggestions in the Notes should not therefore be taken as always applicable.

The teacher should not force on the students a particular way of delivering a poem. The teacher should refrain, if possible, from interrupting the readings to make corrections of pronunciation and inflection.

2. Pictures in Poetry

Part Two in Book Five contains a number of poems which, because of their vivid pictorial quality, should increase the students' ability to visualise, in one form or another, what has been described. In most cases, students are likely to 'see' better when they have been able to listen to a good reading by the teacher. At this point, it is worthwhile emphasizing the importance of the teacher's role as poetry reader. Many a well-planned lesson has failed because of the teacher's inability to present a poem with the sensitivity it deserves. Two or three poems can often be read to create the right atmosphere for a lesson in which the aim is to encourage the students to sketch or paint from the imagination. It would be helpful if the teacher shows interest in the way the readers have presented the poem(s). Once this atmosphere has been achieved, the creative work can begin. Illustrations of a high standard should not be expected and the tendency should always be to praise, rather than to condemn, especially when it is obvious that there has been some effort. No piece of original work should be given any kind of numerical mark, or, indeed, "marked" at all.

3. The Poet as Storyteller

A majority of the poems to be found in Part Three of Book Five should provide good material for discussion and a skilful teacher should also be able to use some of them as examples before a lesson devoted to the students' own original writing. The success of the poetry-writing lesson will depend primarily upon the atmosphere which the teacher has succeeded in creating and maintaining. S/he should, for example, do everything s/he can to prevent untimely interruptions from outside the room. S/he might read some poems to the class at the beginning of the lesson to put the students into the right frame of mind. S/he should be ready to give advice freely, whilst, at the same time, remaining patient with work, which may, perhaps, be rather crude. Lessons of this type, if they are arranged regularly, will almost certainly help to improve both written and spoken English and the teacher will be able to see how concentration on the creative approach to poetry has increased the students' interest in it.

The amount of discussion which will follow the teacher's readings will vary according to the interest and ability of the class and according to the poems that have been read. Although in many instances questions have been suggested in the Teaching and Learning Notes and Guide, a teacher who wishes to maintain interest will avoid the dissection and explanation of every line, unless he feels this to be vitally necessary.

TEACHING AND LEARNING NOTES AND GUIDE
BOOK FIVE

NOTE: *When explanations of words and phrases are given, these refer to the meanings within the context of each particular poem. In other contexts, they may have other meanings.*

The Explanations are given in the order in which the words and phrases occur in the poem concerned.

Explanation of Selected Terms
The following are explanations of selected terms which readers will come across in this book.

Sonnet: A sonnet is a poem of fourteen decasyllabic lines (ten syllables per line) or, rarely, octosyllabic (eight syllables per line) lines. Sonnets can be composed of an octave (eight lines) expressing one phase of an idea, and a sestet (six lines) expressing another phase of the same idea. The fourteen lines can also be set out in different groupings, for example of twelve and two. A variety of rhyme schemes are used.

Ballad: A ballad is a poem or song which tells a story, usually in short stanzas (verses) and often with a refrain (a phrase repeated at intervals, usually at the end of each stanza).

Rhyme: Similar sounds in two or more words, especially at the ends of lines of poetry.

Traditional: Something (usually knowledge) which is passed from generation to generation, not necessarily in written form.

Blank Verse: This is written in iambic metre and does not seek to rhyme at the ends of lines.

PART ONE: POEMS TO SPEAK

FUNERAL SONG

A choral arrangement can be made of this lament for a dead princess. An octet of mixed 'light' and 'dark' voices might speak the first five lines of each verse. The whole class in unison can take the sixth line in each verse; a quartet of mixed voices can take the seventh line and the eighth line can be a duet in each case.

Verse 1
As the coffin passes by, let us sing so that we are heard far and wide.

Verse 2
Nature is no longer able to boast of her possessions, since the most beautiful possession of all is dead. No one, therefore, will be able to resist joining in the lament for the princess's death.

Verse 3
Even the beasts and the spirits of the woods will join in the funeral song.

fauns: spirits; protectors of shepherds.
knell: the bell sounded at a funeral.
nymphs: goddesses supposed to inhabit trees.
sylvans: spirits of the woods.
tenor: the purport; the meaning.

A MORISCO

A Morisco is a traditional dance and is usually known as a Morris Dance.
Group A (mixed 'light' and 'dark' voices) could speak Lines 1, 2, 5, 6, 9, 10, 13, and 14. Group B (mixed 'light' and 'dark' voices) could take lines 3, 4, 7, 8, n, 12, 15, and 16, and both groups combined could read the last four lines of the poem in unison.

ART THOU GONE IN HASTE?
In the first verse, Group A ('light' voices) could speak the first and third lines, whilst an individual student, or the teacher, takes the second and fourth. Group B ('dark' voices) may speak lines 5 and 6, and Groups A and B, together, the seventh and eighth lines. In verse two, Group A could take Lines 1 and 3, and Group B, lines 2 and 4. Group A could then speak line 5, Group B, line 7, and the soloist lines 6 and 8. The last two lines of the poem might be taken in unison by the whole class. ('Ce!' pronounced 'see'.)

THE BLACKSMITHS
This poem provides excellent consonantal practice. A 'cumulative' and then a 'sequential' arrangement could be tried so as to give the maximum individual practice.

Lines	Cumulative	Sequential
Line 1	All the class in unison	
Line 2	One Student	Student 1
Line 3	Two Students	Student 2
Line 4	Three Students	Student 3
Line 5	Four Students	Student 4
Line 6	Five Students	Student 5
Line 7	Six Students	Student 6
Line 8	Seven Students	Student 7
Line 9	Eight Students	Student 8
Line 10	Nine Students	Student 9
Line 11	Ten Students	Student 10
Line 12	Ten Students	Student 10
Line 13	Nine Students	Student 9
Line 14	Eight Students	Student 8
Line 15	Seven Students	Student 7
Line 16	Six Students	Student 6
Line 17	Five Students	Student 5
Line 18	Four Students	Student 4
Line 19	Three Students	Student 3
Line 20	Two Students	Student 2
Line 21	One Student	Student 1
Line 22	All the class in unison	

swart: dark-complexioned.
changelings: the young smiths.
shanks: the parts of the legs between the knees and the ankles.

HUNTING SONG
A suggested choral arrangement of this song is as follows.

Verse 1	
Lines 1-4	The teacher narrates
Line 5	All the class in unison
Verse 2	
Lines 1 and 2	The teacher narrates
Lines 3 and 4	Soloist (preferably a girl)
Line 5	All the class in unison
Verse 3	
Lines 1-4	A soloist
Line 5	All the class in unison
Verse 4	
Lines 1-4	The teacher narrates
Line 5	All the class in unison
Verse 5	
Lines 1-4	The teacher narrates
Line 5	All the class in unison

winds: blows.
brushing: the fox has a tail worth procuring.
He flies the Rout: he heads the hunters.
all spur and switch: their horses are being urged on.
Reynard: the name given to foxes.

MADRIGAL
A madrigal was a type of love song very popular in sixteenth and seventeenth century Europe. It is suggested that half the class reads lines 1-4 and the other half reads lines 5-8. Line 9 can be read by a soloist, lines 10 and 11 by another soloist, and the last line by all the students in the class, in unison. The poem is not intended to be serious and should be spoken light-heartedly.

bereave her jewel: to deprive her of the monkey (which is dying).

THE DEATH OF ADMIRAL BENBOW
This poem can be arranged as follows:

Verse 1	
Lines 1 and 2	Soloist
Lines 3 and 4	Soloist.
Lines 5 and 6	Group A (octet of 'light' voices)
Lines 7 and 8	Group B (octet of 'dark' voices)
Verse 2	
Lines 1 and 2	Soloist
Lines 3 and 4	Soloist
Line 5	Group A
Line 6	Group B
Lines 7 and 8	Groups A and B together
Verse 3	
Lines 1 and 3	Group A
Lines 2 and 4	Soloist
Lines 5-8	Soloist (as above)
Verse 4	
Lines 1 and 2	Soloist
Lines 3 and 4	Soloist
Line 5	Group A
Line 6	Group B
Lines 7 and 8	Groups A and B together
Verse 5	
Lines 1 and 2	Soloist
Lines 3 and 4	Soloist.
Lines 5 and 6	Group B
Line 7 'he says'	Group B
Verse 6	
Lines 1 and 2	Group A
Lines 3 and 4	Group B
Lines 5-8	Soloist
Verse 7	

Lines 1 and 2	Group A
Lines 3 and 4	Group B
Lines 5-8	Soloist

A discussion and some questioning can follow the reading.

Suggested questions
1. What rank did Benbow hold in the Navy?
2. What did his captains do before the fight?
3. Why did they do it?
4. What were the names of the ships that opposed the French?
5. What happened to Benbow?
6. What request did Benbow make after being wounded?
7. Why did he want to be placed on the quarter deck?

A final reading by the teacher, or a student who reads excellently, can complete the lesson.

SEA SHANTY
In each verse, two different small groups could say the first and third lines, whilst lines 2 and 4 are spoken by the whole class in unison.

OLD JOE IS DEAD AND GONE TO HELL
Group A (mixed voices) could read Line 1 of each verse of this old sea-shanty; Group B could read line 3 of each verse and the whole class could speak lines 2 and 4 in unison.

hazing: overworking, bothering.

ONE FRIDAY MORN
This well-known sea shanty can be arranged for choral speaking and then, perhaps, sung. The teacher can narrate most of the shanty, whilst different students speak the parts of the captain, the mate, the cook, and the cabin-boy. The refrain which follows each verse can be said, and later sung, by the whole class in unison.

TARANTELLA

A preliminary reading by the teacher should illustrate to the class the marked rhythmic difference between the first and second verses of this well-known poem. The first verse should be spoken quickly throughout, the second slowly, with due attention paid to the long [ɔːə] sounds.

A suggested choral arrangement is as follows.

Verse 1	
Lines 1 and 2	Soloist
Line 3	Whole class in unison
Line 4. 'and the tedding'.	Group A ('light' voices)
Line 4. 'and the spreading'	Group B ('dark' voices)
Line 5	Group A
Line 6	Group A
Line 7	Group B
Line 8	Groups A and B together
Line 9.	Whole class in unison
Lines 10 and 11	Soloist
Line 12	Groups A and B, together
Line 13	Soloist 2
Line 14	Soloist 3
Line 15	Group B
Line 16 'and the'.	Group A
Line 16. 'hip! hop! hap!'	Soloist 1, 2, 3, separately
Line 17	Group A
Line 18	Group A
Line 19	Soloist 4
Line 20	Soloist 5
Line 21	Soloist 6
Line 22	Soloist 7
Line 2	Group A
Line 24	Group B
Line 25. 'and the'.	Group A
Line 25. 'ting, tong,	Soloists 8, 9, 10, separately (emphasising

tang'.	the sound 'ng' as in 'long')
Line 25. 'of the guitar'.	Group A
Lines 26-28	Whole class in unison
Verse 2	
Lines 1-3	Group B. Long [ɔ] sounds; forlornly
Line 4	Group A
Line 5	Group A
Line 6	Soloist 11, deeply
Line 7. 'In the walls'.	Group C (three 'dark' voices)
Line 7. 'of the halls'.	Groups C and D (five 'dark' voices)
Line 7. 'where falls'.	Groups C, D, and E (three more 'dark' voices)
Line 8	Group B
Line 9	Groups A and B
Line 10	Soloist 11
Line 11	Group B
Line 12. 'of the far water-fall'.	Groups A and B
Line 12. 'like doom'.	The whole class in unison, very deeply

tarantella: a very fast, whirling dance common to Southern Italy.
tedding: spreading of the straw.
hoar: frosty.
Aragon: the name of a river.

THE HIGH SONG
The class can be divided into two halves. One half might read the first two lines and the other half the second two lines of each verse. The reading should be quiet and with a feeling of patience and inevitability. 'The High Song' is the music which has been played and sung to mark the deaths of the 'men and women'.

lute: a musical instrument common between the fourteenth and seventeenth centuries, rather like a guitar.

FULL FATHOM FIVE
This song appears in Shakespeare's play, *The Tempest*, Act I, Scene 2. Ariel sings the song to a young man named Ferdinand after he has been shipwrecked. Ferdinand has been mourning for his father, whom be believes to have been drowned in the shipwreck. The father is not actually dead, but in the play Shakespeare wishes, at this point, to make the young man believe that this is so. At the same time, not wishing the blow to fall too harshly, he makes his character, Ariel, soften the force of what is actually a lying message. Ferdinand's father, therefore, although reported to be dead, has been transformed into something beautiful and rich, and, beneath the sea, the nymphs ring a bell to mourn his passing.

The song (in one verse only) can be arranged for speaking as follows.

Lines 1 and 3	Group A ('light' and 'dark' voices)
Lines 2 and 4	Group B ('light' and 'dark' voices)
Lines 5 and 6	The teacher or a student
Line 7	Group A
Line 8	Group B
Line 9	The whole class in unison

The change of rhythm which occurs at the line, 'But doth suffer a sea-change', should be carefully observed.

O MISTRESS MINE
Another of Shakespeare's songs, this time from the play, *Twelfth Night*. Group A (an octet, perhaps, of mixed voices) could read the first two lines of each verse; Group B (an octet of mixed voices) could read lines 4 and 5 of each verse and lines 3 and 6 in both verses could be spoken by the whole class in unison.
The theme of this poem is the importance of making the best use of present time, rather than waiting for the future.

THE GYPSY LADDIE
After a preliminary reading by the teacher, the following choral arrangement could be adopted.

Verse 1	
Lines 1-4	Narrator (the teacher)
Lines 5 and 6	The whole class in unison
Verse 2	Soloist 1
Verse 3	Narrator
Verse 4	Soloist 1
Verse 5	Soloist 2
Verse 6	Soloist 1
Verse 7	Soloist 2
Verse 8	Narrator
Verse 9	Soloist 2

During two or three readings of the poem, different students can speak the parts of the Squire and the lady.

squire: chief landowner and gentleman of a district.
gipsum: gypsy.

HIS GRANGE, OR PRIVATE WEALTH
Different soloists can speak the alternate lines 2, 4, 6, 8, etc., until the end of the poem. The short lines 1, 3, 5, 7, etc. ('Though Clock'; 'A Cock'; 'I have', etc.) can be said alternately by the two halves of the class.

grange: country-house. *Prew*: a name (Prunella).
creeking: clucking. *miching*: thieving. *trasy*: spaniel dog.

THE GARDEN SEAT
At night the spirits of all the people who once sat on the garden seat return to sit on it once again.
The teacher, or perhaps three different students, can read the first two lines of each verse. Line 3 of each verse can be read by one half of the class and line 4 of each verse by the other half.

THE BELL-MAN
Many years ago, it was the custom in different parts of the world for watchmen to patrol villages, towns, and cities. Their job was to protect the sleeping inhabitants against criminals, fires, and other dangers. At intervals, each watchman would ring a bell and

Poems to Enjoy, Book Five (4th Ed, 2015)

call out the time, with some such cry as, 'Ten o'clock on a fine night, and all's well!'
Herrick's poem refers to the cry of such a watchman, or 'bellman'.
It is suggested that the whole class speaks this poem in unison and that a reading of it might round off a choral speaking lesson.

Benedicite: expressing a blessing. Invoking God's help against murders.
mischances: unlucky happenings.

POOR OLD HORSE
Individual students may read the first four lines of each verse, whilst the refrain is said by the whole class in unison.

linsey woolsey: coarse woollen fabric.
sprouts: a type of green vegetable.

SONG FROM THE SHIP
Group A (mixed voices) could read the first three lines of each verse; Group B (mixed voices) could speak lines 4, 5, and 6 of each verse; Groups A and B together could speak line 7 of each verse and the last line in each case could be taken by the whole class in unison.

wanton: sportive.
dolphin: a sea mammal like a porpoise.
bark: ship.
azure: blue.
Triton: son of Poseidon, the sea-god.

SONG
The first six lines of each verse of this poem can be read by a different individual student, whilst the last line in each verse can be spoken by the whole class in unison.
The poem was written at sea during the Anglo-Dutch war in 1665, just before a battle.

indite: write.
Muses: the Nine Sister Goddesses of learning and art.
Neptune: God of the Sea.
azure main: blue sea.
Whitehall: the offices of the various Government departments in London.

THE MAID OF THE MOOR
A suggested choral arrangement of this poem is as follows:

Verse 1	
Lines 1, 2, 4, and 5	Group A (mixed voices)
Lines 3 and 6	The whole class in unison
Verse 2	
Lines 1, 2, 5 and 6	Group A
Line 3	Group B ('light' voices)
Line 4	Group C ('dark' voices)
Line 7	The whole class in unison
Verse 3	*As for Verse 2.*
Verse 4	*As for Verses 2 and 3.*

primrose: a pale yellow English flower.
violet: a bluish-purple wild and garden flower.

THE HAPPY HEART
The theme is that wealth does not necessarily bring happiness with it. It is better to be contented without riches, than to be troubled with them.
In the first verse, Lines 1 and 3 can be spoken by two different soloists; lines 2 and 4 by the whole class in unison; line 5 by Group A (a quartet of 'light' voices); line 6 by Groups A and B (a quartet of 'dark' voices) together; line 7 by Group A; line 8 by Group B; line 9 by Groups A and B together, and line 10 by the whole class speaking in unison. The same arrangement can apply to the second verse.

apace: quickly.

ALL FOR LOVE
The theme is that youth is preferable to Fame, and that Fame, if achieved, is only worthwhile if it makes the poet's dear one feel that he is worthy to love her.
The poem could be spoken throughout by two groups of mixed voices. Group A could speak Lines 1 and 2 of each verse. Group B could join Group A, so that the last two lines of each verse are spoken by the two groups together.

myrtle: an evergreen shrub with beautiful, sweet-smelling leaves. In the Mediterranean, myrtle was symbolic of love and immortality.
ivy: Dedicated to the roman god Bacchus and the Greek god Dionysius. Used to crown poets in Ancient Rome. Believed to aid fertility. A symbol of fidelity.
laurel: In ancient Greece laurel wreaths were awarded to victors, both in athletic competitions and in poetic meets; in Rome they were symbols of martial victory. In common modern idiomatic usage a laurel wreath refers to any victory. The expression 'resting on one's laurels' refers to someone relying entirely on long-past successes for continued fame or recognition, where to "look to one's laurels" means to be careful of losing rank to competition.

The implication of lines 3 and 4 of the first verse is that it is better to be young than famous.

THE BELLS OF SHANDON
The poet has heard the sound of bells in different parts of the world, but none sounded so pleasant to him as those of his own home town.
Different individual students can be given the opportunity of reading a verse each of the poem.

sublime: wondrously impressive.
brass tongues: the clappers of the bells.
Vatican: the residence of the Pope in Rome.
Notre-Dame: a famous Cathedral in Paris.
the dome of Peter: St. Peter's Cathedral, Rome.

minarets: the turret of a mosque from which the call to prayer is chanted.

THE THREE WISE MEN OF GOTHAM
In this poem it is suggested that the teacher, or a student who has had previous warning, read the lines belonging to Old Care, i.e. Lines 1, 3, and 7 of verse one; lines 2, 4, and 5 ('"Tis Jove's decree'), and 6 of verse two; Lines 1, 3, and 7 of verse three. The other lines of the poem could be given to a trio of speakers, the members of which could be changed each time the poem is read so as to bring the maximum number of students into the lesson.

ballast: material used to steady the boat.

ODE
The class can be divided into three groups of mixed voices. Each group may speak one verse of the poem in unison. The 'music-makers' referred to are all the men and women in the world, and the main theme of the poem is that each age is a preparation for the next.

Nineveh: the ancient capital of Assyria.
Babel: the ancient city of the Bible in which a tower was to be built to reach to heaven. The building of it, however, ceased because the language of the builders was confounded and they were scattered.

MARCHING ALONG
The poem refers to the English Civil War which took place between the forces of the King, the Royalists or Cavaliers, and the forces of Parliament, the Parliamentarians or Roundheads, in the seventeenth century. Sir Byng and Rupert (the King's nephew) were Royalists; Hampden and Pym were well-known Parliamentarians.

The following arrangement is suggested:

Lines 1 and 2	Group A ('mixed' voices)
Lines 3 and 4	Group B ('mixed' voices)
Line 5	Group A

Line 6	Group B
Lines 7 and 8	Groups A and B together
Lines 9 and 10	1st Soloist
Lines 11 and 12	2nd Soloist
Lines 13, 14, and 15	Groups A and B together
Lines 16 and 17	Group A
Lines 18 and 19	Group B
Line 20	Group A
Line 21	Groups A and B together
Lines 22 and 23	The whole class in unison
Line 24	Group A
Line 25	Group B
Lines 26 and 27	The whole class in unison

crop-headed: most Parliamentary soldiers had their hair cut short. The Royalists wore long hair.
carles: churls; surly fellows.
paries: talk.
obsequies: funeral.
snarls: speaking ill-temperedly.

SONG OF THE BOWMEN OF SHU
For an intelligent class with previous experience of choral work. A first reading by the teacher should illustrate to the class that poetry of this type should be spoken naturally and easily, in the manner of everyday speech.

A suggested arrangement is as follows:

Line 1	The whole class in unison	
Line 2	'and saying'	The whole class in unison
Line 2	'When shall we get back to our country?'	Group B (octet of 'dark' voices)
Lines 3 and 4		The whole class in unison
Line 5		Group A (octet of 'light' voices)

Poems to Enjoy, Book Five (4th Ed, 2015) 158

Line 6	'when anyone says'	Soloist 1
Line 6	'Return'	Group A
Line 6	'the others are full of sorrow'	Group B
Line 7	'sorrowful minds'	Group A
Line 7	'sorrow is strong'	Group B
Line 7	'we are hungry and thirsty'	Groups A and B together
Line 8		The whole class in unison
Line 9		Group B
Line 10	'We say'	Group A
Line 10	'Will we be let to go back in October?'	Group B
Lines 11 and 12		The whole class in unison
Line 13		Soloist 2
Line 14	'Whose chariot?'	Soloist 3
Line 14	'The General's'.	Soloist 4
Lines 15 and 16		Group B
Line 17		Group A
Line 18	'The generals are on them'.	Group A
Line 18	'The soldiers are by them'.	Group B
Lines 19 and 20		Groups A and B together
Line 21		Group A
Line 22		Group B
Line 23		Group A
Line 24		Group A
Line 25		The whole class in unison.

The theme of the poem is the sadness of exiles far from their homes and familiar scenes. This element of sadness should appear in spoken readings of the poem.

Poems to Enjoy, Book Five (4th Ed, 2015)

AN INDIAN SUMMER DAY ON THE PRAIRIE
The class can be divided into four groups. Group A ('light' voices); Group B ('light' voices), Group G ('dark' voices), and Group D ('dark' voices). Each group can read a verse of the poem. Group A, verse one; Group B, verse two; Group C, verse three; and Group D, verse four. The poem contains a series of pictures describing the sun at various times of the day. These pictures should be kept in mind when the poem is being spoken. The different possible choral effects might be discussed by students and teacher after a first reading and variations can be added to subsequent readings.

baleful: destructive, malignant.

PART TWO: PICTURES IN POETRY

JAQUES' SEVEN AGES OF MAN
This famous speech from Shakespeare's play, *As You Like It*, is excellent material for illustration work providing the teacher ensures that the students understand the archaic language of the blank verse. The poem is best spoken by the teacher himself and if the class is interested and has had some previous experience, students can be encouraged to take turns to mime the characters described.
pard: leopard.
bubble reputation: a reputation which doesn't last very long.
capon: chicken.
saws: sayings.
pantaloon: a feeble old man.
sans: without (French language).

BREAK, BREAK, BREAK
The monotonous breaking of the sea on the rocks echoed by the first lines of verse one and four ('Break, break, break') recalls sad memories to the poet. The teacher's readings should reflect this sadness. The scenes described (the breakers thundering on to the rocks; the fisherman's children at play; the boy-sailor singing in his boat in the bay; the passing ships) are suitable for illustration.
haven: harbour.

TROPIC RAIN
The theme is that there is room in the world for suffering and joy, sadness and happiness. The thunder can make people afraid, but it brings with it rain, often beneficial to Man.
After the teacher's reading, the students could be asked to sketch or paint a tropical storm scene.
levin: lightning.

OZYMANDIAS
Shelley's sonnet should be read twice to the students. A discussion and some questioning could then follow.

Suggested questions
1. What did the traveller describe to the poet?
2. To what did the 'shatter'd visage' belong?
3. Whom did the sculptured legs and visage represent?
4. What 'works' had Ozymandias succeeded in creating? (None. Hence the inscription.)
5. What surrounded the pieces of sculpture?
6. Whose was 'The hand that mock'd them and the heart that fed'?

visage: face.

After the discussion, a further reading can be given and then the students may be encouraged to sketch or paint the scene described.

THE ICE-CART
The poet, uncomfortable in the oppressive heat of his office, dreams he is in the Polar regions, swimming with the seals.
After listening to two readings by the teacher, the students could be asked to illustrate the imagined scene.

in a trice: in a moment. *berg*: iceberg.

THE LISTENERS
Two readings straight through by the teacher can be followed by a discussion and some questioning.

Suggested questions
1. Imagine you are the Traveller. What can you hear as you stand outside the door?
2. Who listened as the Traveller knocked?
3. What message did the Traveller leave for the listeners?
4. What did the listeners hear when the Traveller left?
5. What caused 'the sound of iron on stone'?

After the discussion, the students can be encouraged to illustrate any one aspect of the poem (e.g. the listeners in the house peering at the Traveller; the Traveller and his horse waiting outside the door; the lonely house in the moonlight).

champed: chewed noisily. *hearkening*: listening.

ON FIRST LOOKING INTO CHAPMAN'S 'HOMER'

The author of this poem, John Keats, was lent by his friend, Charles Cowden Clarke, a copy of Chapman's translation of Homer's epic poem The Iliad. He was so impressed after reading it that he composed the poem on the same night and gave his friend a copy of it on the next day. The thrill Keats experienced was so great that, in the poem, he compared it to the thrill felt by an explorer or an astronomer after he has made a new discovery. After two readings by the teacher, the poem can be discussed and the discussion can be followed by a final reading.

realms of gold: this is not to be translated literally. Keats means that he has read a good deal of fine literature.
goodly states and kingdoms: this, again, should not be treated literally, but should be interpreted as, 'authors and the work that they have written'.
bards: poets.
Apollo: the god of poetry.
wide expanse: the epic form. Homer used it magnificently and was therefore 'ruler' of it.
surmise: suspicion that something exists.

DOCKS

The vocabulary is rather difficult in this poem and new words should be explained in the context of sentences in a separate lesson, before the poem is read. Once the unfamiliar words are known, the poem provides very suitable material for a lesson which begins with two or three readings by the teacher, continues with a short discussion and concludes with some sketching and painting by the students.

Suggested questions
1. When do the ships usually come into the docks?
2. What do they have to pass through to get in?
3. What happens when the gates move?
4. How are the estuaries and foreshores kept free of silt?
5. When do the flood-tides occur?
6. What do the pumps do?
7. What are the cylinders moved by?
8. What is the granite for?
9. What is the refuse shifted by?
10. What can be found in the warehouse?

lintels: the wood across the top of the gates.
quoins: corners of the gates.
top-gallant yards: spars of masts.
spanker-vang: a rope holding a sail.
dolphin-striker: a short spar.
bowsprit: the spar running forward from a ship's bow.
dray: a low cart.
prores: prows.
neap-tides: tides in which high water is at its lowest.
algae: seaweed.
mussels: shell-fish.
littoral drift: driftwood, etc. from the sea.

SONG OF THREE GORGES
Three pictures are described in this short poem. They are the view from the twelve Hills of the Witches of the mountains and the sky; the boat moored to the quay at Nan-pin and the final resting places of Ch'u Yuan and Yu. The students can be asked to illustrate one of these pictures after two readings by the teacher.

myriad: a vast number.

FRAGMENT (Page 60)
This vivid description of a waterfall provides suitable material for illustration after the teacher's reading. The fall is described in human terms (i.e. it is *personified*). It 'elbows down rocks' and 'shoulders' its way over the precipice. It seems to be in almost continual agony.

THE LYCHEE
If the new vocabulary can be introduced to the class in a previous lesson, this poem may be read straight through without comment.

lustrous: shining.
lambent: quietly brilliant.
saffron: orange-coloured.
peerless: unequalled by any other.
pre-eminent: beyond all other fruit.

THE MUSIC OF THE SEA
This imaginative little poem could be read in conjunction with 'Break, Break, Break'. The mood is, of course, a happier one. The poet believes that in the 'rich and wondrous' sounds of the sea he can hear echoes of the past. The one picture imagined (the poet with one ear to the sand, listening to the sea) can be illustrated by the class.

THE KINGFISHER
For illustration, particularly if kingfishers can be seen in the pupils' own district.

Verse 1
The Kingfisher is brightly coloured like a rainbow and, just as a rainbow follows rain, so the Kingfisher lives near lonely pools of water and trees that shed water from their branches.

Verse 2
Because of its glorious colours the Kingfisher is good enough to live with Peacocks and 'Before the windows of proud Kings'.

Verse 3
The Kingfisher, however, is not a vain bird, and the poet, like the bird, is happiest in a quiet place near a pool and a tree.

THE VILLAGE SCHOOLMASTER
This extract from Oliver Goldsmith's long poem, 'The Deserted Village', should be read twice to the class and then be followed by a discussion and some questioning.

Suggested questions
1. Where was the school situated?
2. Why does Goldsmith call the school 'a noisy mansion'?
3. What did the pupils do when the schoolmaster made a joke?
4. What happened when he frowned?
5. What made him severe?
6. What did the people in the village think of him?
7. What happened when he was defeated in argument?

furze: a spiny shrub.
unprofitably gay: i.e. because it was outside the school.
the boding tremblers: the pupils who saw by his face that the schoolmaster was, perhaps, going to be angry.
cypher: do sums.
presage: predict.
gauge: measure.
rustics: simple village people.

THE KITTEN AND THE FALLING LEAVES
Wordsworth describes a colourful picture in simple language. The teacher's readings can be followed by sketching and painting work by the pupils.

eddying: whirling round and round.
sylph: spirit of the air.
plaudits: applause.

I STOOD TIPTOE
The poem should be read quietly to the class by the teacher when appropriate classroom conditions can be guaranteed. After the

second reading, sketching and painting can begin. The results and the means used to achieve them may afterwards be discussed and compared.

diadems: crowns (in this context, the 'dew').
the green: the meadows.

FROM PIPPA PASSES
This vivid description of a sunrise should be read twice to the class by the teacher, before he encourages the students to sketch or paint it.

HELEN'S TOWER
The tower was built by a son in memory of his mother. The tower wishes that it could, by continuing to stand, perpetuate that memory until the end of the world.

The poem should be read twice, straight through. Little explanation should be necessary.

FROM THE RIME OF THE ANCIENT MARINER
For illustration by the students after two readings by the teacher.

hoary: grey and old.

THE BULL
Before the first reading, new words can be discussed with the class and written on the blackboard in the context of suitable sentences. The poem might then be read aloud twice by the teacher. After the readings, the students may be asked to illustrate the poem from memory. Individual paintings or drawings can be examined in a follow-up lesson and, after a further reading, the teacher might lead the class to a discussion of the poem by means of some of the questions suggested below.

Suggested questions
1. How does the bull feel?
2. Why is it difficult to see him?
3. Explain the meaning of 'careless' (line 8) as it is used in this extract.
4. What is urging the bull to seek a fight?

5. How is the horse affected?
6. Explain the phrase, 'aerial summit.' (line 24).

lusty: vigorous. *negligent*: neglectful.
enticing: desirable. *feigns*: pretends.
gored: stabbed; pierced. *impetuous*: impulsive, forcible.
cleaves: passes through. *straitened*: narrow. *eddies*: whirlpools.

ON THE SEA
Keats' sonnet can be read twice to the class, without preliminary explanation.

Hecate: a goddess with power over earth, heaven, and sea.
cloying: over-sweet.

THE BELFRY
This poem is suitable for illustration after the poem has been read twice to the class. A discussion can follow the readings and immediately precede the sketching and painting.

Suggested questions
1. What are the walls of the tower like?
2. How does the light enter the tower?
3. Why does the girl hang back?
4. Where are the children trying to get to?
5. What makes the children's fingers 'tighter press'?
6. How do the reapers know that the day's work is finished?

sexton: an official who has care of a church, bell-ringing and grave-digging.
plangent: a lamenting sound.

HORSES ON THE CAMARGUE
The Camargue is a stretch of land in southern France upon which graze many wild cattle and horses. The men who are responsible for looking after the cattle ride very speedy white horses of a type which is well-known to be characteristic of the district.
Vocabulary difficulties should be dealt with in a previous lesson, so that the teacher's two readings can be left uninterrupted.

Neptune's car: the chariot of the god of the sea.
Mistral: a very strong, cold wind experienced in the parts of France near the Mediterranean Sea.
verges: the borders.
herbage: herbs.
the white-crested fillies of the surge: the breakers.
their Master's trident: Neptune's trident (three-pronged spear).
their sisters of the sea: the breakers.

The frequent comparisons made between the horses and the waves of the sea should be noted.

SHE WALKS IN BEAUTY
This poem should be read to the class twice. No explanation or comment should be necessary.

THE KRAKEN
The Kraken is a mythical monster of the sea. After the teacher's readings, the students can allow their imaginations to picture its form and shape as they sketch and paint. The vocabulary difficulties should be cleared up in a previous lesson.

abysmal: bottomless. *millennial*: thousand-year old.
grot: cave.
polypi: sea-anemones.
winnow: fan (with their fins).
battening upon: eating greedily, thriving at the expense of others.
the latter fire: the great fire before the end of the world.

A FEAST OF LANTERNS
This poem is suitable for illustration after the teacher's readings.

myriad argosies: vast number of ships.

THE NILE
Two readings by the teacher of this poem about Egypt's great river, should prepare the students for illustration work. After this is finished, a further reading can complete the lesson.

THE RELEASE
This poem pictures the contrast between the monotony of the man's daily work in the factory and his release from this monotony at night, when he is free to play the music he loves. The teacher's reading should make clear the contrast between the first and second verses. There should be little need for questions and explanation, if the reading is sufficiently effective.

RAIN AT DAWN
This poem should be read by the teacher or the students. Questions or explanations are unnecessary.
plain: complaint.

ARTISTS
The poem should be read to the class straight through without preliminary explanation.

bodkin: a thick needle. *to boot*: as well.

PART THREE: THE POET AS STORYTELLER

THE LADY OF SHALOTT
This poem can occupy two or three periods. After it has been divided suitably into episodes, each episode can be read separately with questions following the reading, as for 'Paul Revere's Ride' in Book Tour. Before this work begins, the teacher can summarise the story briefly.

Part I
The approach to Camelot is described and reference is made to the island of Shalott and the Lady who lives there.
The Lady of Shalott lives under a curse in her castle on the island of Shalott overlooking Camelot. If she once looks 'down to Camelot', the curse will take effect. To avoid this, therefore, she watches the scenes and people outside through a mirror that 'hangs before her all the year'. One day, however, the knight, Sir Lancelot, passes by, singing. The Lady sees him, looks directly out of the window and immediately the mirror cracks and the curse comes upon her. Under the power of the curse, the lady comes out of the castle, enters a boat, 'beneath a willow left

afloat' and is borne away down the river to die, as the boat reaches Camelot. As the boat carrying the dead lady drifts by, the people of Camelot, 'knight and burgher, lord and dame', see her and wonder who she is. Lancelot (unknowingly responsible for the lady's death) comments on the loveliness of her face and asks God's grace for her.

Suggested questions
1. Which crops grow on either side of the river?
2. What does the lady's home look like from the outside?
3. How do the reapers know there is a lady in the castle?
4. What do the reapers call the lady?

wold: an open tract of upland country.
aspens: trees of a particular kind (trembling poplars).
shallop: a light boat.

Part II
The poet describes the Lady sitting in her room, busily weaving. The curse prevents her from looking out of her window, other than through a mirror. Although she is able to see many different people and scenes in the mirror, she is nevertheless tired of the curse.
'"I am half sick of shadows," said the Lady of Shalott.'

Suggested questions
1. How does the lady occupy herself in her room?
2. What does the curse prevent her from doing?
3. Is the lady in love?
4. What people will appear on the 'web' she is weaving?

churls: rustics. *pad*: (here) a horse.

Part III
Sir Lancelot appears riding by. His apparel and equipment are described. When the Lady hears his singing, she is tempted, leaves her loom and looks out of the window. The curse immediately comes upon her.

Suggested questions
1. How far away from the Lady's castle is Sir Lancelot?
2. What design is on his shield?
3. With what does the poet compare Lancelot's bridle?
4. How could Lancelot be heard as he rode down to Camelot?
5. What happened when the Lady saw Sir Lancelot in her mirror?
6. What happened in her room after she looked down to Camelot?
7. What did the Lady see when she looked out of the window?

brazen greaves: brass armour for Lancelot's leg below the knee.
baldric: sash for the shoulder.

Part IV
The Lady comes down from her room, steps into the boat, loosens the chain and drifts away down 'the broad stream' towards Camelot. As the boat drifts along, she sings one last song before dying. When the boat reaches Camelot, Lancelot and the people see her and read her name, which is inscribed on the prow of her boat.

Suggested questions
1. What did the Lady do when she found the boat?
2. Towards which place did the boat drift?
3. What happened to the lady after she had finished her song?
4. What happened when the boat reached Camelot?
5. What inscription did the people of Camelot find on the boat's prow?

seer: a person who sees into the future.
burgher: a freeman (citizen) of a borough.

A final reading of the poem by the teacher should complete the examination of it.

OLD MAN TRAVELLING
This poem, following out Wordsworth's theories which were expressed in practical form in the *Lyrical Ballads*, is one of great

simplicity. The character of the Old Man, nevertheless, is well-drawn and benefits from the poet's measured judgment.

THE HIGHWAYMAN
After the first reading by the teacher, the poem can be read and discussed in sections. A preliminary summary of the story should not in this instance be necessary.

Part I
The highwayman rides up to the inn and attracts the attention of Bess, the landlord's daughter. Tim, the ostler, who is himself in love with Bess, and later betrays the highwayman, listens to their conversation. The highwayman asks Bess to wait for him at moonlight and then gallops 'away to the west'.

Suggested questions
1. When did the highwayman come riding to the inn?
2. How did he attempt to attract Bess's attention?
3. What was Bess doing whilst waiting for the highwayman?
4. Where was the ostler?
5. What was he doing?
6. When did the highwayman say he would be back?
7. In which direction did he ride?

ostler: a person who attends to horses at an inn.

Part II
Tim, the ostler, informs the authorities of the highwayman's planned return to the inn. The soldiers take up their positions and bind a musket beside Bess with the muzzle pointing towards her breast. They then settle themselves to wait for the highwayman's return. At midnight, the highwayman's horse can be heard approaching. Bess hears him and warns him by firing the musket, which kills her. The highwayman turns and gallops away, but later hears of Bess's act and returns to the inn, only to be shot down on the high road.

Suggested questions
1. What did the soldiers do to Bess?
2. What could Bess see through her window?

3. How had Bess been tied by the soldiers?
4. What did Bess do when she heard the highwayman approaching?
5. What did the highwayman do when he heard the shot?
6. What action did he take when he heard of Bess' sacrifice?

The lesson can be completed with a further reading by the teacher. The last two verses in the poem could, if desired, be arranged for choral speaking.

THE SOLDIER

Clare's sonnet tells of the thoughts of the shepherd who has become a soldier and is far from his home. Letters are very precious to him because they remind him of his village and his friends.

The poem can be read straight through with only the minimum of preliminary explanation.

THE SHAWL

The teacher's readings of the complete poem can be followed by a discussion and questioning.

The maiden's patient and loving work which produces the lovely shawl receives a ridiculously small monetary payment.

Suggested questions
1. Where was the shawl made?
2. What scenes did the maiden weave into the shawl?
3. What did the maiden's mother tell her?
4. Why was the maiden joyful?
5. When was the shawl finished?
6. Do you think the maiden was paid enough?

A final reading by the teacher may complete the lesson.

MEETING AT NIGHT

The feeling of mystery about the 'meeting' will be better preserved if this poem is read straight through without comment, or explanation.

THE DESTRUCTION OF SENNACHERIB
The Biblical story of Sennacherib is told in Kings II, Chapters 18 and 19. Sennacherib, King of Assyria, attacked the people of Judah in the reign of Hezekiah; but 'it came to pass that night, that the angel of the Lord went out, and smote in the camp of the Assyrians an hundred fourscore and five thousand: and when they arose early in the morning, behold, they were all dead corpses.
So Sennacherib king of Assyria departed, and went and returned, and dwelt at Ninevah.'
The poem should be read to the class by the teacher and followed by a short discussion.

Assyria: an ancient nation in the Tigris Valley.
cohorts: troops.
deep Galilee: the Sea of Galilee (now in Israel).
waxed: became.
Ashur: one of the largest Assyrian towns.
Baal: a god of the Phoenicians.
Gentile: a person who is not a Jew.

PARTING AT MORNING
To be read without comment.

JAFFAR
A discussion with some questioning can follow the teacher's readings of the poem.

Suggested questions
1. What position had Jaffar held?
2. What did Haroun order after Jaffar's death?
3. Why did he order it?
4. Who ignored Haroun's order?
5. Why did Mondeer disobey Haroun?
6. What did Mondeer do when he disobeyed Haroun?
7. What did Haroun do when he heard that Mondeer had disobeyed his orders?
8. What did Mondeer say when the mutes bound his arms?
9. What did Haroun do next?
10. Why did he do it?

11. What gift did he offer Mondeer?
12. What did Mondeer do with Haroun's gift?

Vizier: a minister.
scimitar: a curved sword.
caliph: a ruler, successor of Mohammed.

STILL WATERS
This little story of a boasting river can be read straight through, without comment.
The Till is a sluggish tributary of the River Tweed in Scotland.

GOLIATH
This poem recounts the Biblical story of the mighty giant-warrior, Goliath, who is killed by the young shepherd-boy, David, with a mere pebble from a sling.
The teacher should give a brief summary of the story before reading the poem two or three times to the class. Some questions can be asked and a discussion can take place after the reading.

Suggested questions
1. What message did Goliath shout to both armies?
2. Whom did Goliath see when he turned round?
3. What was the shepherd-boy doing?
4. Why did Goliath shut his eyes?
5. What did Goliath do when the voice warned him?
6. Where did 'the pebble-messenger' come from?

empyrean: the sky.
cormorant: a greedy sea-bird.
the untroubled green: the green fields.
mote: a particle of dust.
Souffriere: a West Indian volcano.

FROM SOHRAB AND RUSTUM
This extract from Matthew Arnold's long poem describes the fight between Sohrab and Rustum. Sohrab, the son of the Persian hero, Rustum, has joined the forces of the Tartars and has already, by his prowess, become their champion. When Rustum and Sohrab meet in single combat during a battle between the

Tartars and the Persians, neither knows the identity of the other and, unhappily, Rustum kills his son.

The teacher should read the extract to the class twice and then encourage a discussion.

Suggested questions
1. What happened at the beginning after Rustum had spoken?
2. With what does Arnold compare the two warriors as they rush at one another?
3. Why was there a tremendous noise when they fought each another?
4. Why did the poet say that he believed the sun and stars were taking part in the conflict?
5. With what different weapons did Sohrab and Rustum fight?
6. What caused the two armies to 'quake for fear'.
7. What caused Sohrab to step back?
8. What made Sohrab drop his shield?

kindled at his taunts: became angry at his (Rustum's) taunts.
unnatural conflict: i.e. unnatural because it was taking place between father and son.
they twain: the two of them.
shore away: cut away.
quak'd for fear: shivered with fright.

HOW THEY BROUGHT THE GOOD NEWS FROM GHENT TO AIX
The poem can be read twice to the students without preliminary explanation. During the second reading, members of the class can speak the lines of the watch, the echo of the wall ('Speed!') and the lines spoken by Joris.
Questioning and a discussion can follow the reading.

Suggested questions
1. What did the rider who narrates the story do to make his horse gallop faster, after riding out of the gates?
2. What time of day was it when the three began their ride?
3. What was the time when they reached Lokeren?
4. Which rider was the first to drop out?

5. How did Joris know that Aix was in sight?
6. At what point in the poem did Joris's horse die?
7. What refreshment was given to the horse, Roland, at the end of the journey?

postern: gate. *a whit*: a bit.

KUBLA KHAN

In the year 1797, Coleridge, the author of this poem, was living in a lonely farm-house in Exmoor in England. One evening, after taking a drug for an indisposition, he fell asleep in his chair whilst reading a book commonly referred to as "Purchas's Pilgrimage". The following passage appears in the section of the book that he was reading: 'In Xanadu did Kublai Kan build a stately Palace, encompassing sixteene miles of plaine ground with a wall, wherein are fertile Meddowes, pleasant springs, delightfull streames, and all sorts of beasts of chase and game, and in the middest thereof a sumptuous house of pleasure.'

When Coleridge awoke, this factual description of Kubla Khan's palace still remained in his mind and it so impressed him that he immediately set his imagination to work to produce the series of vivid pictures contained in the poem.
If the new vocabulary can be explained in a previous lesson, this poem is best read through twice with the minimum of comment.

Kubla Khan founded the dynasty of the Mongols in China and built the capital city, Pekin (now 'Beijing').
sinuous rills: winding streams.
cedarn: of or relating to the cedar (tree).
dulcimer: a stringed musical instrument.

AFTER BLENHEIM

This poem is a comment on the futility of war. The so-called victory of the English over the French resulted in the deaths of many thousands of men.

A discussion and some questioning can follow two readings by the teacher.

Suggested questions
1. What did Wilhelmine see her brother do beside the river?
2. What object had the boy found?
3. What was the battle fought for?
4. Why didn't Kaspar really believe that the battle was a great victory?
5. How can you tell that Kaspar did not believe that the battle was a victory?

THE ROSE
Again, little explanation of this poem should be necessary. The theme is that material things cannot flourish without the help of heaven.

bards: poets.

FROM MY LOST YOUTH
Six separate groups in the class can take turns to speak the last two lines of each verse, during the second reading of the poem by the teacher.
The poet is in reflective mood, recalling the scenes and incidents of his youth. This mood should, if possible, be captured in the reading.

Hesperides: the sisters who guarded in their beautiful gardens the golden apples given to Hera, wife of the Greek god, Zeus, by Gaea.

THE DEATH OF SAMSON
Questioning by the teacher will help the class to understand this extract from John Milton's long poem, 'Samson Agonistes'.

Two readings by the teacher can be followed by questions similar to the following:
1. At what time of day did the messenger enter the city?
2. What rumour did the Messenger hear?
3. Why was Samson to be brought forth?
4. Where was the spectacle to take place?
5. In which part of the 'theatre' did the Messenger stand?
6. When was Samson brought forward?

7. How was he dressed?
8. How did the people greet him?
9. When was he led between the pillars?
10. What did Samson do after speaking to the spectators?

timbrels: tambourines.

THE EASTERN GATE
The poor man, despite the pleas of his wife and his love for his family, determines to leave his home to seek his fortune.

The poem should be read twice to the class without comment. A short discussion could then follow the reading.

LA BELLE DAME SANS MERCI
The knight is wooed by the beautiful but strange lady, and is saddened when she lulls him to sleep and disappears without warning. He is then in her thrall (i.e. in bondage to her) because he is unable to stop thinking of her.

A discussion might follow the teacher's readings.

Suggested questions
1. Where is the knight?
2. Why is he 'haggard' and 'woe-begone'?
3. Where did the knight meet the lady?
4. Where did the lady take the knight?
5. What did she do at this place?
6. What did the knight dream?
7. Why was he waiting on the hill-side?

sedge: a type of plant, usually to be found near a lake or stream.
meads: meadows. *grot*: grotto, cave

THE CAP AND BELLS
This fantasy-poem recounts the story of the jester who, firstly, despatches his soul to his lady-love and this is refused. Secondly, he sends his heart to her, but this, also, is refused. Lastly, he sends the badges of his office (the cap and the bells) to her and then dies. The lady then accepts the three gifts.

The poem should be read to the class twice without comment.

THE GALLEY OF COUNT ARNALDOS
A short discussion and some questioning might follow the second reading of this poem.
Suggested questions
1. What visions haunt the poet?
2. Which particular legend haunts him the most?
3. What did Count Arnaldos see?
4. What did the Count ask the helmsman?
5. What reply did the helmsman give?

Silent reading by the students may complete the lesson.

A LAKE AND A FAIRY BOAT
This poem can be read straight through without preliminary explanation.

gossamers: extremely fine spider-threads.

THE MERMAID
This poem could, perhaps, be read to the class to provide the students with a theme for their own original writing.
sate: sat. *jaspers*: forms of quartz.

THE ENCHANTED ISLAND
A discussion and some questioning can follow after this poem is read twice to the class.

Suggested questions
1. Where did the poet sail?
2. What did the mermaid do every evening?
3. When did the island appear?
4. What would happen if a stone were to be thrown on the island?
5. What makes the mermaid and the island disappear?
Silent reading of the poem by the class can follow the discussion.

turbid: muddy.
dell: a small valley shaded by trees.

dulcet: sweet. *fanes*: temples.

THE ENCHANTED SHIRT
After two readings by the teacher, the poem can be divided into suitable sections and each section read and discussed separately.

Verses 1-5
The king declares that he is sick, although, in fact he is perfectly well. He insists, nevertheless, that he is sick and all the doctors who visit him, and cannot cure him, lose their heads. At last, two famous doctors arrive. One has devoted himself to his work during the whole of his career; the other has become wealthy by devoting his time to patients who are rich. Both doctors examine the king.

Suggested questions
1. How do we know that the king was not really sick?
2. What happened to the doctors who could not cure the king?
3. What did the two new doctors do when they examined the king?

Verses 6-13
The wise doctor is hanged for stating that the king is perfectly healthy; the other doctor suggests that if the king can sleep for one night in the shirt of a happy man, then he will recover. The king therefore sends couriers to find such a man. Eventually they discover the happy beggar.

Suggested questions
1. What happened to the wise doctor who suggested that the king was perfectly healthy?
2. What made the two men by the roadside miserable?
3. Where did the couriers find the beggar?

Verses 14-18
The couriers ask the beggar for his shirt, but he confesses gaily that he doesn't possess one. At this news and the other news brought to him by the couriers, the king changes his attitude and begins to rule so wisely that he himself and his people become very much happier.

Suggested questions
1. Why couldn't the beggar lend the couriers his shirt?
2. What reports did the couriers bring to the king?
3. What happened to the king as a result of these reports?

Silent reading of the poem might complete the lesson.

BISHOP HATTO
After briefly summarising the story, the teacher should read the poem to the class twice. Various sections of the poem could then be read separately and discussed.
During a famine in the Rhineland, Bishop Hatto invited a large number of poor people to come to his barn for food. When they were all inside the barn, he locked the doors, set fire to the building and burnt them all to death.
On the following morning, as he entered the hall of his palace, he was horrified to see that rats had eaten his own portrait out of its frame. Men then came to warn him that a vast number of rats (ten thousand) was advancing on his castle. Hoping to escape them, the Bishop fled across the Rhine to his tower on an island in the river. Scarcely, however, had he begun to rest when the mad screams of his cat warned him that the army of rats had drawn near. The Bishop fell to his knees and began to pray, but the rats poured in through all the windows and doors, killed the Bishop and gnawed his bones. The rats had been sent to do judgment on the Bishop and thus he paid for his crime.

Verses 1-6
The reasons for the famine are explained (the summer and the autumn had been very wet and the corn had rotted away). The poor people ask the Bishop for help, he invites them to his barn, sets fire to it and the people are burnt to death. The Bishop justifies this act by claiming that the country should be obliged to him for getting rid of a number of people who would have eaten the corn.

Suggested questions
1. Why was there a famine?
2. What had made the corn go rotten?
3. What did the poor people want from the Bishop?
4. What did the Bishop offer the people?
5. What did the Bishop do when the people were all in the barn?
6. What reason did the Bishop give for his action?

granaries: large buildings in which corn is usually stored.
i' faith: certainly, truly.

Verses 7-11
The Bishop returns to his palace and sleeps happily that night. Next day, however, he finds his portrait has been eaten; he is warned of the approaching rats and he decides to leave for his castle on the island.

Suggested questions
1. What did the Bishop find when he awoke on the next morning?
2. What did the man from the farm have to report?
3. What message did the second man bring?
4. What did the Bishop decide to do when he heard that the rats were approaching?

Verses 12-18
The Bishop seeks shelter in his tower on the island, but is caught by the rats and killed.

Suggested questions
1. What did the Bishop do when he reached his tower?
2. What startled him just as he began to rest?
3. How did the rats get into the tower?
4. What did the Bishop do when he saw the rats?
5. Why had the rats been sent to kill the Bishop?

His beads he did tell: He counted the beads of his rosary, whilst praying.

Silent reading of the poem should follow the readings and discussion.

ON A CERTAIN LADY AT COURT
This admirable lady has only one fault, if it can be called such; modesty.
A short discussion can follow the teacher's second reading of the poem.

GET UP AND BAR THE DOOR
The teacher can narrate this poem, whilst individual students read the parts of the goodman and his goodwife and of the two gentlemen.
A discussion and some questioning can follow the readings.

Suggested questions
1. When was the goodwife making her puddings?
2. Why did the goodwife refuse to bar the door?
3. What pact did the goodman and the goodwife make between them?
4. Why did the two gentlemen wonder whether the house was rich, or poor?
5. What did the guests eat?
6. What did the strangers propose to do?
7. Who protested?
8. What was the result of the protestation?

Martinmas: the feast of Saint Martin (11th November).

THE PARROT
The old bird has been away from its birthplace, Spain, for many years. After living in a cage in another country where it 'lived and chattered many a day', it becomes at last blind and apparently dumb so that it 'scolded, laughed and spoke no more.' Just before its death, however, the parrot is spoken to by a visitor from Spain. The bird is so overjoyed to hear again the tongue of its native land that it speaks once again and replies to the visitor in Spanish.
The poem can be read to the class without preliminary explanation.

ABOUT THE EDITOR

Verner Bickley is an educationist who has led international education projects in Singapore, Burma, Indonesia, Japan, Saudi Arabia and Hong Kong. For two years, he was Chairman of Directors of the East-West Centre in Hawaii and, for ten years, was Director of the Centre's Culture Learning Institute. He has served as an adjudicator in speech and drama festivals in several countries and as President of the English-Speaking Union in Hawaii and Chairman of the English-Speaking Union in Hong Kong. He has lived and worked in Hong Kong since 1983.

Specialising in institutional linguistics, language pedagogy and international education, Dr Bickley has written extensively on language and culture and on language learning and teaching. He has served as announcer and actor in radio and TV programmes broadcast in several Asian and Pacific countries. His voice was heard regularly over the NHK in Tokyo, the Burma Broadcasting Service, Radio Republic Indonesia and Radio Malaya where he broadcast from Singapore as newsreader and as actor and narrator in radio drama, as well as in programmes for schools and colleges.

Among the dozens of scripts he has written were five in a series on the use of poetry in the language class, broadcast in BBC radio's "Listen and Teach" series. Twenty scripts written by Dr Bickley for the Japan Broadcasting Company were broadcast as the television series, "How English Works".

His books include *Reading and Interpretation* (co-authored), *Reading and Understanding* (co-authored), *A New Malayan Songbook* (co-authored), *Easy English*, *Cultural Relations in the Global Community*, *Searching for Frederick* (an autobiographical-biographical narrative), *Language and the Young Learner in Hong Kong*, and *Forward to Beijing*. The first volume of his autobiography entitled, *Footfalls Echo in the Memory*, was published in 2010. The second volume, *Steps to Paradise and Beyond: Hawaii to China, Saudi Arabia, Hong Kong and elsewhere*, was published in 2013.

Born in Cheshire, England, Dr Bickley received two bachelor's degrees from the University of Wales, befor earning an M.A. degree in education there. He was made a Licentiate of the Royal Aademy of Music (Speech and Drama) in 1955 and a Licentiate of the Guildhall School of Music and Drama in the same year. He was awarded a PhD in socio-linguistics by the University of London in 1966. He is a Fellow of the Royal Society of Arts.

Employed by the British Council for twelve years, he moved from university teaching and advisory assignments to the position of English Language Officer for Japan and First Secretary in the Cultural Department of the British Embassy in Tokyo.

Dr Bickley was founding Director of the Hong Kong Government's Institute of Language in Education (which was incorporated into the Hong Kong Institute of Education after his retirement) and an Assistant Director of Education.

Dr Bickley was made a Member of the Order of the British Empire in 1964.

ABOUT PROVERSE HONG KONG

Proverse Hong Kong, co-founded by Gillian and Verner Bickley, is based in Hong Kong with long-term and growing regional and international connections. Verner Bickley has led cultural and educational centres, departments, institutions and projects in many parts of the world. Gillian Bickley has recently concluded a career as a University teacher of English Literature spanning four continents. Proverse Hong Kong draws on their combined academic, administrative and teaching experience as well as varied long-term participation in reading, research, writing, editing, indexing, reviewing, publishing and authorship.

Proverse has published novels, novellas, fictionalized autobiography, non-fiction (including biography, history, memoirs, sport, travel narratives), single-author poetry collections, children's, teens / young adult and academic books. Other interests include diaries, and academic works in the humanities, social sciences, cultural studies, linguistics and education. Some Proverse books have accompanying audio texts. Some are translated into Chinese.

Proverse welcomes authors who have a story to tell, wisdom, perceptions or information to convey, a person they want to memorialize, a neglect they want to remedy, a record they want to correct, a strong interest that they want to share, skills they want to teach, and who consciously seek to make a contribution to society in an informative, interesting and well-written way. Proverse works with texts by non-native-speaker writers of English as well as by native English-speaking writers.

The name, "Proverse", combines the words "prose" and "verse" and is pronounced accordingly.

THE PROVERSE PRIZE

The Proverse Prize, an annual international competition for an unpublished book-length work of fiction, non-fiction, or poetry, was established in January 2008. Unusually for a competition of this nature, it is open to all who are at least eighteen on the date they sign the entry form and without restriction of nationality, residence or citizenship.

The objectives of the Proverse Prize are: to encourage excellence and / or excellence and usefulness in publishable written work in the English Language, which can, in varying degrees, "delight and instruct". Entries are invited from anywhere in the world. Long-listed writers to date include writers born or resident in Andorra, Australia, Canada, Germany, Hong Kong, New Zealand, Nigeria, Singapore, Taiwan, The Bahamas, the PRC, the United Arab Emirates, the United Kingdom, the USA.

CO-FOUNDERS
Dr Verner Bickley, MBE and Dr Gillian Bickley.
To celebrate their lifelong love of words in any form, as readers, listeners, performers, teachers, academics, writers, editors, indexers and publishers.

HONORARY ADVISORS (2009-)
Marion Bethel (poet, the Bahamas), Margaret Clarke (academic and translator, UK) David Crystal (linguist and lexicographer, UK), Jonathan Hart (academic and poet, Canada), Björn Jernudd (academic and linguist, Sweden), Edwin Thumboo (academic and poet, Singapore), Olga Walló (novelist, translator, Czech Republic).
HONORARY LEGAL ADVISOR: Mr Raymond T. L. Tse.
HONORARY JUDGES: Anonymous.
HONORARY ACCOUNTANT: Mr Neville Chow.
HONORARY UK AGENT & DISTRIBUTOR: Miss Christine Penney.
HONORARY ADMINISTRATORS: Proverse Hong Kong.

Proverse Prize Winners whose work has already been published by Proverse Hong Kong
2009: Laura Solomon, Rebecca Jane Tomasis
2010: Gillian Jones
2011: David Diskin, Peter Gregoire
2012: Sophronia Liu, Birgit Bunzel Linder
2013: James McCarthy
2014: Celia Claase, Philip Chatting
2015: (Scheduled) Lawrence Gray, Gustav Preller

Summary Terms and Conditions
(for indication only & subject to revision)

The information below is for guidance only. Please refer to the year-specific Proverse Prize Entry Form & Terms & Conditions, which are uploaded, no later than 30 April each year, onto the Proverse Hong Kong website: <www.proversepublishing.com>.

The Proverse e-Newsletter includes ongoing information about the Proverse Prize. To receive current information, email info@proversepublishing.com, requesting to be put on the free Proverse eNewsletter mailing-list.

The Prize
1) Publication by Proverse Hong Kong, with
2) Cash prize of HKD10,000 (HKD7.80 = approx. US$1.00)

Supplementary publication grants may be made to selected other entrants for publication by Proverse Hong Kong.

Depending on the quality of the work in any year, the prize may be shared by at most two entrants or withheld, as recommended by the judges.

In 2016, the entry fee is: HKD220.00 OR GBP32.00.

Writers are eligible, who are at least eighteen on the date they sign The Proverse Prize entry documents. There is no nationality or residence restriction.

Each submitted work must be an unpublished publishable single-author work of non-fiction, fiction or poetry, the original work of the entrant, and submitted in the English language. School textbooks and plays are ineligible.

Unpublished first translations into English (including those already published in the writer's mother tongue) submitted by the author are welcome. The submitted work will not be judged as a translation but as an original work.

Extent of the Manuscript: within the range of what is usual for the genre of the work submitted. However, it is advisable that novellas be in the range 30,000 to 45,000 words); other fiction (e.g. novels, short-story collections) and non-fiction (e.g. autobiographies, biographies, diaries, letters, memoirs, essay collections, etc.) should be in the range, 75,000 to 100,000 words. Poetry / poetry collections should be in the range, 5,000 to 25,000 words. Other word-counts and mixed-genre submissions are not ruled out.

Writers may choose, if they wish, to obtain the services of an Editor in presenting their work, and should acknowledge this help and the nature and extent of this help in the Entry Form.

KEY DATES FOR THE PROVERSE PRIZE IN ANY YEAR
(subject to confirmation and/or change)

Receipt of Entry Fees / Entry Documents	[No later than] 14 April to 31 May of the year of entry
Receipt of entered manuscripts	1 May to 30 June of the year of entry
Announcement of Semi-finalists	July-September of the year of entry
Announcement of Finalists	October-December of the year of entry
Announcement of winner/ max two winners (sharing the cash prize)	December of the year of entry to April of the year that follows the year of entry
Cash Award Made	At the same time as publication of the work(s) adjudged the winner / joint-winners of the Proverse Prize
Publication of winning work(s)	In or after November of the year that follows the year of entry

EDUCATIONAL BOOKS FROM PROVERSE

Jockey, by Gillian Bickley (when Gillian Workman). Hong Kong, 1979. Pbk. 64pp. ISBN-10: 962-85570-3-3; ISBN-13: 978-962-85570-3-5.

Poems to Enjoy: Book 1, Edited by Verner Bickley. HK & UK: 2012. Pbk. 136 pp. (inc. 35 b/w original line-drawings & Teacher's and Student's Notes). With audio CDs. ISBN 978-988-8167-54-8.

Poems to Enjoy: Book 2, Edited by Verner Bickley. HK & UK: 2013. Pbk. 136pp. (inc. 37 b/w original line-drawings & Teacher's and Student's Notes). With audio CDs. ISBN 978-988-8167-51-7.

Poems to Enjoy: Book 3, Edited by Verner Bickley. HK & UK: 2013. Pbk. 166 pp. (inc. 39 b/w original line-drawings & Teacher's and Student's Notes). w. audio CDs. ISBN 978-988-19934-1-0.

Poems to Enjoy: Book 4, Edited by Verner Bickley. HK & UK: scheduled, 2014. Pbk. *c.*174 pp. (inc. *c.*41 b/w original line-drawings & Teacher's and Student's Notes). With audio CDs. ISBN 978-988-8167-50-0.

Poems to Enjoy: Book 5, Edited by Verner Bickley. HK & UK: scheduled, 2015. Pbk. *c.*200 pp. (inc. *c.*36 b/w original line-drawings & Teacher's and Student's Notes). With audio CD(s) / DVD(s). ISBN 978-988-8167-49-4.

Spanking Goals and Toe Pokes: Football Sayings Explained, by T. J. Martin. HK & UK, 2008. ISBN-13: 978-988-99668-2-9.

Teachers' and Students' Guide to the Book and Audio Book, 'The Golden Needle: the Biography of Frederick Stewart (1836-1889)'. Proverse Hong Kong Study Guides. E-book. ISBN-10: 962-85570-9-2; ISBN-13: 978-962-85570-9-7. 24Reader e-book edition (2010), ISBN-13: 978-988-19320-5-1.

FIND OUT MORE ABOUT OUR AUTHORS AND BOOKS

Visit our website
<www.proversepublishing.com>
Visit our distributor's website
<www.chineseupress.com>

Follow us on Twitter
Follow news and conversation:
<twitter.com/Proversebooks>
OR
Copy and paste the following to your browser window and follow the instructions:
https://twitter.com/#!/ProverseBooks

"Like" us on www.facebook.com/ProversePress

Request our E-Newsletter
Send your request to info@proversepublishing.com.

Availability
Most titles are available in Hong Kong and world-wide from our Hong Kong based Distributor,
The Chinese University Press of Hong Kong,
The Chinese University of Hong Kong, Shatin, NT,
Hong Kong SAR, China. Web: chineseupress.com
All titles are available from Proverse Hong Kong
and the Proverse Hong Kong UK-based Distributor.

We have stock-holding retailers in Hong Kong,
Singapore (Select Books),
Canada (Elizabeth Campbell Books),
Principality of Andorra (Llibreria La Puça, La Llibreria).
Orders can be made from bookshops in the UK and elsewhere.
Ebooks
Most of our titles are available also as Ebooks.

www.ingramcontent.com/pod-product-compliance
Lightning Source LLC
Chambersburg PA
CBHW071116160426
43196CB00013B/2587